Relationship Workbook for Couples

Improve Your Communication Skills, Build Better Intimacy, and Overcome Trust Issues for a Deeper Connection

Emily Pope

TABLE OF CONTENTS

INTRODUCTION

Every couple has that moment where they find themselves sitting across from each other, whether it is during a romantic candlelit dinner or a quiet evening at home, and they start wondering, "How did we get here?" It is not always a negative reflection. Sometimes it is a moment of marvel as they reflect on the journey they have embarked on together, the challenges they have faced, the moments of joy they have shared, and the memories they have created. But at other times, it sparks a genuine concern, leading them to question the distance that has somehow crept into their relationship, almost without them noticing. The once fiery passion seems to have dimmed, the conversations have dwindled, and the connection feels fragile. It is in these moments that the true essence of a relationship is put to the test.

Have you ever experienced that sensation, where you stand at a crossroads, unsure of which direction to take, longing for a map or a guide to show you the way? You are not alone. Every relationship, no matter how perfect it seems on the outside, has its moments of doubt, its challenges, and its need for reconnection.

In the age of instant gratification, where everything is just a click away, relationships seem to have become another item on the checklist. Meet someone, fall in love, move in together, perhaps get married, and maybe even have children. It all seems so ... scripted. But what happens when the script ends? When the honeymoon phase is over, and reality sets in?

The truth is that relationships are hard work and require substantial effort. They need understanding, patience, and a lot of love. But in the hustle and bustle of daily life, amidst work pressures, family obligations, and societal expectations, couples often find themselves drifting apart. The conversations become transactional centering on bills, chores, or schedules. The intimacy fades, replaced by the monotony of routine. The laughter, the shared dreams, and those cherished little moments that once brought joy seem to get lost.

This drifting apart is not something couples intend to happen. No one enters a relationship with the hope of eventually becoming strangers sharing the same home. Yet, it happens. External pressures, personal ambitions, or even past traumas can create invisible walls. Over time, these walls become so thick that couples find it hard to break them down. They long for the connection they once had, the understanding they once shared, and the dreams they once built together.

The problem is not the lack of love. It is the lack of understanding, effective communication, and the tools necessary to navigate the intricacies of a relationship in today's ever-evolving world.

Every relationship, much like a ship, encounters storms. Some are foreseeable, while others appear out of the blue. But what if there was a compass, a guide, that could help navigate these tumultuous waters? What if couples had a roadmap to understand each other better, to communicate more effectively, and to rebuild the bridges that have been burned?

The solution is not a magic potion or a one-size-fits-all answer. It is a journey of understanding, introspection, and personal growth. It is about recognizing that every relationship is unique, with its own set of challenges and strengths. Yet, at the heart of every enduring, resilient relationship lies a foundation built on trust, understanding, and mutual respect.

This journey requires effort. It is not about finding faults or playing the blame game. It is about understanding each other's perspectives, acknowledging the pain points, and working together to find a middle ground. It is about rekindling the spark, reigniting the passion, and rediscovering the joy of being together.

But how does one start this journey? It begins by arming oneself with the right tools, knowledge, and a receptive mindset. It also needs one to be open to change, to learning, and to growing together. By understanding that love, in its truest form, is a verb. It is an action, a continuous effort to show up, to understand, and to cherish.

The catalyst for this transformative journey is often a realization, a moment of clarity when couples recognize the drift and feel the urge to bridge the gap. It is the moment when they decide that their love is worth fighting for and that their relationship deserves a second chance. With the right guidance, tools, and mindset, they can not only revive their relationship but also make it stronger, more resilient, and more fulfilling.

Every relationship has its highs and lows, moments of joy and challenges. Picture it as navigating a maze, where every turn feels uncertain, and every path seems daunting. But what if there was a guide, a beacon of light, capable of illuminating the way and making the journey less intimidating?

The solution is not about finding a quick fix or a temporary Band-Aid. It is about embarking on a transformative journey; one where couples delve deep, understanding the intricacies of their bond, the silent whispers, and the unspoken words. It is about realizing that while every relationship has its unique rhythm and melody, the dance of love requires both partners to move in harmony.

Embarking on this path requires commitment. It is not about pointing fingers or dwelling on the past. It is about embracing the present and understanding each other's dreams, fears, and aspirations. It is about reigniting the flame that once burned bright and finding joy in the little, everyday moments.

But where does one begin? By arming oneself with knowledge, understanding, and a willingness to evolve. By acknowledging that love is not just a feeling; it is a conscious decision made daily.

Often, the first step toward this transformation is a moment of epiphany. It is a realization that the bond shared is precious and worth every effort. With the right guidance and mindset, couples cannot only navigate the challenges but also build a relationship that is profound, meaningful, and resilient.

Imagine a world where every disagreement with your partner becomes an opportunity for growth, where every challenge faced together strengthens the bond, and where every shared dream draws you closer. This is not a utopian fantasy; it is a tangible reality that countless couples have achieved, and so can you.

By diving into the pages of this book, you are not just gaining knowledge; you are opening a vault of profound insights that have the potential to transform your relationship. Here is a glimpse of what lies ahead:

- **Clarity:** Understand the underlying dynamics of your relationship, the patterns that play out, and the reasons behind certain reactions or behaviors.

- **Tools for Growth:** Equip yourself with practical exercises, reflective questions, and actionable steps that can be seamlessly integrated into your daily life.

- **Deeper Connection:** Learn the art of truly listening, understanding, and empathizing with your partner, fostering a connection that goes beyond words.

- **Conflict Resolution:** Turn disagreements into constructive conversations, ensuring that every conflict becomes a stepping stone toward a stronger relationship.

- **Shared Dreams:** Discover the power of shared visioning, aligning your dreams, aspirations, and goals, and charting a path forward together.

- **Rekindling Passion:** Reignite the spark, ensuring that the flame of passion, intimacy, and romance never dims.

This is not just another relationship book. It is a journey, a guide, and a companion that will stand by your side, offering wisdom, support, and guidance at every step. Whether you aim to rekindle the flames of romance, navigate through challenging phases, or simply deepen your bond, the insights and strategies in this book can be your guiding light.

One chilly winter evening, I found myself sitting across from a couple celebrating their golden anniversary — fifty years of togetherness, yet their eyes still sparkled with the same affection and admiration. Curiosity led me to ask them about the secret behind their enduring bond. Their response was simple but profound: "Understanding, patience, and a willingness to grow together." That conversation was one of the many that inspired the creation of this book.

Over the past two decades, I have had the privilege of working with countless couples, each with their own unique stories, challenges, and dreams. Whether it was newlyweds embarking on their journey of marital bliss or couples celebrating decades of togetherness, certain patterns began to emerge. Relationships, like any other aspect of life, require effort, understanding, and the right tools.

The insights shared in this book are not just theoretical. They are distilled from real-life experiences, countless hours of research, and interactions with couples from various walks of life. They have been tried, tested, and proven to be transformative.

While academic qualifications can lay a foundation, it is the hands-on experience, the stories shared in confidence, the tears wiped away, and the moments of realization that truly shape the essence of this book. It is a culmination of lessons learned, both personally and professionally, and a testament to the belief that every relationship, no matter how challenging, possesses the potential to blossom into something beautiful.

Imagine a relationship where misunderstandings are rare, where both partners feel genuinely heard and valued, where challenges become stepping stones for growth, and where love deepens with each passing day. It might sound like an idyllic dream, but it is a reality that many couples have achieved and continue to enjoy. And the best part? It is entirely within your reach.

Every relationship undergoes its share of ups and downs, moments of joy, and periods of challenge. However, armed with the right tools and mindset, you can navigate these waters gracefully and emerge even stronger. The strategies and insights presented in this book are designed to guide you toward this very objective. They are not abstract concepts but practical steps that can be seamlessly integrated into your daily life. By putting them into practice, you will not only enrich your relationship but also unearth a deeper connection with your partner.

This is not about quick fixes or superficial changes. It is about laying a strong foundation, understanding each other's needs, and forging a bond capable of withstanding the test of time. It is about cultivating a relationship that is not merely about surviving but thriving.

Every moment spent in a relationship is precious. It is a tapestry woven from memories, emotions, and shared experiences that shape our lives. But time, as they say, waits for no one. The longer we delay addressing the issues in our relationship, the deeper they entrench themselves. Small misunderstandings can escalate into major conflicts, and unresolved feelings can fester, leading to resentment and emotional distance. Before we know it, the chasm between us and our partner widens, making reconciliation all the more challenging.

But here is the silver lining: The present moment is a gift, an opportunity. Right now, you have the chance to make a change, to take a step toward a brighter, happier future with your partner. The insights and strategies in this book are your compass, guiding you toward a relationship filled with understanding, love, and harmony.

However, these tools are only as effective as your commitment to put them into action. The potential for a fulfilling relationship is within arm's reach, but it necessitates action. Every day you wait is another day lost to misunderstandings, hurt feelings, and missed opportunities for connection.

The journey to a stronger, more loving relationship starts now. Not tomorrow, not next week, but today. Because in the grand tapestry of life, it is the choices we make in the present that shape our future.

Every relationship is unique, just as every individual is. Nevertheless, beneath the surface of each love story, there are universal truths and shared experiences that resonate with many. Perhaps you have picked up other books, seeking answers, only to find generic advice that did not quite align with your situation. Maybe you have sought counsel from friends and family, only to realize that while their intentions were good, their advice was not tailored to you and your partner.

This book is different. It is not just a collection of theories or abstract concepts. It is a culmination of real-life experiences, insights, and actionable strategies tailored for modern couples. It understands the nuances, the silent struggles, the unspoken dreams, and the deep-seated fears that many couples face. It recognizes the beauty of individuality within a partnership and celebrates the power of two individuals coming together with a shared purpose. Whether you are in the early stages of your relationship, celebrating decades together, or somewhere in between, this book speaks directly to you. It is not about changing your partner or fitting into a mold. It is about understanding, growth, and building a bond that can endure the test of time.

You might have moments of doubt, moments when you question whether things will ever change or if you are on the right path. But remember, every relationship has its ups and downs. What truly matters is the commitment to journey together, to learn, adapt, and grow. With this book by your side, you are not alone. You have a guide, a companion that understands and supports you every step of the way. As you turn the pages, you will find echoes of your own experiences, aspirations, and dreams. You will discover tools and strategies that resonate with your unique journey. This is not just another relationship book; it is *your* relationship book. It is a testament to the belief that with understanding, effort, and love, every couple has the potential to craft their own beautiful love story.

CHAPTER 1:
SETTING THE STAGE

In this opening chapter, we embark on a deep exploration of the fundamental aspects of relationships, delving into the complex dynamics of love and partnership. Mutual respect and understanding, often regarded as simple terms, will be unpacked to unveil their profound influence on the well-being of a relationship. As you conclude this chapter, you will have acquired a heightened awareness of the foundational principles that sustain your bond and will be better prepared to cultivate and safeguard it. Let us begin this enlightening journey together, strengthening the core of our connections.

The Building Blocks of Relationships

On a chilly December evening, Sarah and Mark found themselves seated across from each other at a dimly lit café. They had been dating for a few months, and as the steam from their cups of cocoa rose, so did a question in Sarah's mind: Why do some relationships thrive while others falter? As they would come to realize over the years, the answer lies in the fundamental principles of love, mutual respect, and understanding.

Have you ever wondered what makes love so powerful? At the heart of every thriving relationship lies the intricate dance of attachment styles. Some of us exhibit secure attachment, harboring confidence in our partner's love and support. Others may display anxious attachment, constantly seeking reassurance, or avoidant attachment, valuing independence above all. Recognizing and understanding these styles is the first step in navigating the complex labyrinth of human connections.

Nevertheless, attachment styles are merely the surface of a much deeper sea. Beneath the surface, mutual respect and understanding form the bedrock of lasting love. Picture a relationship as a house. Without a sturdy foundation, even the slightest tremor can cause the walls to crumble. Similarly, in the absence of mutual respect, even minor disagreements can escalate into major conflicts. Respect is about valuing your partner's feelings, beliefs, and boundaries. It is about listening with an open heart and responding with kindness. Understanding, on the other hand, serves as the window to your partner's soul. It entails diving deep into their fears, dreams, and aspirations. It involves walking in their shoes and seeing the world through their eyes. When we truly understand our partners, we create a safe space for vulnerability and personal growth.

So, as you embark on this journey of exploration, remember Sarah and Mark's evening at the café. Remember that at the core of every successful relationship are the principles of love, mutual respect, and understanding. As you flip through the pages of this workbook, may you discover practical insights and exercises aimed at strengthening these foundations.

Tip: Take a moment to reflect on your attachment style and discuss it with your partner. Understanding each other's styles can pave the way for deeper connection and empathy in your relationship.

The Evolution of Relationships

The beginning of a relationship often resembles a whirlwind romance. The world takes on a brighter hue, every song on the radio feels like it was written for you, and every moment spent apart feels like an eternity. This is the honeymoon phase, where everything is new, exciting, and full of promise.

However, as days turn into months and months into years, that initial spark may start to fade. It is not that the love is gone, but rather, the dynamics of the relationship shifted. The late-night conversations become morning routines, and the spontaneous weekend getaways transform into planned family vacations.

This evolution is natural and expected. Relationships, like everything in life, go through different seasons. The key lies in recognizing that each season, whether it is the passionate beginning or the comfortable middle, has its own beauty and challenges.

For instance, as a relationship matures, couples may face challenges such as navigating career changes, financial pressures, or even starting a family. These challenges, while daunting, offer opportunities for growth, understanding, and deeper connection. They put the relationship's foundation and resilience to the test.

Adaptability becomes crucial during these times. It is about understanding that change is inevitable and that growth often arises from discomfort. It is about learning to navigate choppy waters together, holding onto each other even when the currents attempt to pull you apart.

Keep in mind that every relationship will face its storms. However, it is not the absence of challenges that defines a successful relationship; rather, it is how you face them together. Embrace the natural evolution, cherish the memories, and remain open to growth and change.

Tip: Establish a routine of regularly checking in with your partner about your relationship's evolution. Discuss the highs, the lows, and the in-between moments. This open communication will ensure that you both are on the same page and moving forward together.

The Interplay Between Mutual Respect and Understanding

Picture walking into a room filled with people speaking different languages. The cacophony of unfamiliar sounds can be overwhelming, and the odds of miscommunication are significant. Now, imagine a relationship devoid of mutual respect and understanding. It is much like that room, where two people are speaking different emotional languages, resulting in confusion and conflict.

Mutual respect is the cornerstone of any healthy relationship. It is the silent agreement that both partners are equal, and that their feelings, thoughts, and opinions matter. It is about valuing each other's individuality and celebrating the differences. When we respect our partners, we create a safe environment where both can freely express themselves without the fear of criticism or mockery.

But respect alone is not enough. Understanding functions as the bridge that connects two individuals. It is the effort to truly get to know your partner, to delve deep into their psyche, and to empathize with their experiences. It entails active listening, not just with your ears, but with your heart. When we strive to understand our partners, we see the world from their perspective, making it easier to navigate challenges together.

Have you ever had a disagreement with your partner where you felt unheard or misunderstood? Now, reflect on a moment when you felt truly seen and understood by them. The difference in those experiences lies in the presence (or absence) of mutual respect and understanding.

Practical Exercise: Dedicate some time with your partner to discuss your values, beliefs, and experiences. Listen actively, without interrupting or judging. This simple exercise can pave the way for deeper understanding and connection.

Tip: Remember, mutual respect and understanding are ongoing processes. It is essential to revisit these principles regularly, ensuring that they remain at the forefront of your relationship.

Exercise: Relationship Reflection

Strengths: Reflect on the strengths of your relationship. What are the qualities and experiences that make your bond unique and strong?

_____

_____

_____

_____

Weaknesses: Consider the areas where you both feel there is room for improvement. What are the challenges you have faced or are currently facing?

_____

_____

_____

_____

Opportunities: What are the potential areas for growth in your relationship? Think about the experiences or activities you would like to explore together.

_____

_____

_____

_____

Threats: Are there external factors or internal dynamics that could pose challenges to your relationship? Identify them.

_____

_____

_____

_____

Discussion & Reflection: After filling out the above sections individually, come together and discuss your answers. Note down areas where your thoughts align and where they diverge.

Areas of Alignment	Areas of Divergence

Action Steps: Based on your reflections and discussions, what are the steps you both agree to take to strengthen your relationship further?

_____

_____

_____

_____

CHAPTER 2:

UNDERSTANDING LOVE LANGUAGES

In this chapter, we embark on a journey to explore the concept of Love Languages - a unique lens through which we perceive acts of love and affection. Grasping the nuances of these languages and recognizing their impact on our relationships can be a game-changer. By navigating the shifts and evolutions in how we and our partners express love, we open doors to deeper connections and fewer misunderstandings. Delve into this chapter not only to uncover your own love language but also to gain insight into and resonate with your partner's. Together, let us unlock the secret code to more genuine affection and connection.

The Basics of the Love Languages

In a quaint little town, two lovers sat under a tree, exchanging gifts. Anna handed Tom a handwritten letter, pouring out her deepest feelings. Tom, in return, gave Anna a beautiful bracelet. Both gestures were acts of love, yet they spoke different languages.

The renowned Dr. Gary Chapman, in his groundbreaking work, introduced the world to the concept of the "Five Love Languages." These are unique ways through which individuals express and receive love. Understanding these languages is similar to unlocking a secret code in one's heart. Let us explore each of these languages in depth:

Words of Affirmation: For some, verbal expressions of love mean the world. A simple "I love you," a compliment or words of appreciation can make their day. It is all about articulating feelings.

Acts of Service: Actions often speak louder than words for people who resonate with this love language. Cooking a meal, helping with chores, or any act of service shows them you care.

Receiving Gifts: It is not about materialism; it is the thought and effort behind the gift that matters. Whether it is a special occasion or just because a thoughtful gift can speak volumes.

Quality Time: Undivided attention is the key here. Spending time together, having deep conversations, or simply enjoying each other's company is their way of feeling loved.

Physical Touch: A hug, a kiss, holding hands — for some, physical touch is their primary way of expressing and receiving love.

Imagine the depth of connection you can achieve when you understand your partner's primary love language. It is like tuning into a radio frequency that plays your favorite song. Anna's letter to Tom was her way of expressing love through "Words of Affirmation," while Tom's gift was his "Receiving Gifts" language in action.

Tip: Take some time to reflect on those moments when you felt the most loved. What was happening? Was it a word, an act, a gift, time spent, or a touch? Identifying these moments can provide valuable insights into your primary love language.

The Impact of Love Languages

In the initial stages of their relationship, Emily would often surprise Jake with thoughtful gifts — a book she thought he would love, a scarf in his favorite color, or even tickets to a concert. She believed these gestures represented the ultimate expressions of her love. Jake, on the other hand, would spend hours talking with Emily, sharing stories, dreams, and even the most mundane details of his day. To him, quality time symbolized the pinnacle of intimacy.

It was not until a friend introduced them to Dr. Gary Chapman's concept of love languages that they began to realize the root of some of their misunderstandings. Emily's primary love language was "Receiving Gifts, while Jake's was "Quality Time." They were both expressing love, but in ways the other did not entirely recognize.

Understanding love languages can have a profound impact on a relationship. It is not just about knowing how you express love, but also how your partner perceives and receives it. When couples can identify and cater to each other's primary love language, they can bridge communication gaps and foster a deeper connection.

Nevertheless, misunderstandings can arise when love languages are misinterpreted. For instance, a partner whose primary love language is "Words of Affirmation" might feel unloved if they do not frequently hear words of appreciation, even if their partner is constantly performing acts of service for them. Similarly, someone who values "Physical Touch" might feel distant if their partner is not as physically affectionate, even if they are spending quality time together.

The beauty of understanding love languages lies in its ability to offer a roadmap to navigate these potential pitfalls. By recognizing and valuing each other's love languages, couples can ensure that they are not just expressing love, but that it is being received in the way they intend.

Practical Exercise: Allocate an evening with your partner to discuss your primary love languages. Reflect on times when you felt most loved and see if they align with these languages. Then, brainstorm ways in which you can better cater to each other's love languages in your daily lives.

Adjusting to Shifts in Love Languages

L ife is a journey of constant evolution. We grow, learn, and adapt to the myriad of experiences that come our way. Just as we evolve as individuals, our love languages can also shift and transform over time. The way we express and receive love in our twenties might differ from our approach in our forties or fifties. Life events, personal growth, and even challenges can influence these shifts.

Take, for instance, a couple welcoming their first child. The demands and joys of parenthood might mean that "Acts of Service" become more significant than "Quality Time." Or imagine a partner going through a personal crisis; during such times, they might find comfort in "Words of Affirmation" more than "Physical Touch."

Recognizing these shifts is crucial. It is not about clinging to the past but rather embracing the present. It is about understanding that love, in its essence, remains constant, but its expression can vary.

So, how can couples effectively navigate these changes?

Open Communication: Regularly check in with each other about how you feel loved and appreciated. Be open to the possibility that your primary love language might have changed.

Stay Curious: Approach your relationship with a sense of curiosity. Explore new ways to express love and see how they resonate with your partner.

Practice Empathy: Understand that shifts in love languages often stem from deeper emotional needs. Be empathetic and supportive as your partner navigates these changes.

Seek Balance: While it is essential to cater to your partner's evolving love language, do not neglect your own emotional needs. Find a balance that ensures both partners feel loved and valued.

Practical Exercise: Reflect on significant life events or changes in the past few years. Have they influenced how you express or receive love? Discuss these reflections with your partner and explore ways to adapt to each other's evolving love languages.

Exercise: Love Language Assessment

Understanding each other's love language can profoundly impact the way you communicate love and appreciation. This assessment is designed to assist you in identifying your primary love language and guide you on how to accommodate your partner's love language.

1. Your partner has had a long day at work. You:

a) Give them a long, comforting hug.

b) Spend quality time with them, listening to their day.

c) Surprise them with their favorite meal.

d) Offer to handle the household chores for the evening.

e) Write them a heartfelt note expressing your support.

Answer: [____]

2. It is your anniversary. You feel most loved when your partner:

a) Buys you a thoughtful gift.

b) Plans a day out for just the two of you.

c) Cooks a special meal for you.

d) Takes over your responsibilities for the day.

e) Tells you how much they cherish the time spent together.

Answer: [____]

3. When you are feeling down, you appreciate it most when your partner:

a) Holds you close.

b) Sits with you and listens.

c) Brings you a small gift to cheer you up.

d) Helps out with tasks you are struggling with.

e) Reassures you with encouraging words.

Answer: [____]

Scoring System:

Count the number of times you chose each letter:

a) Physical Touch: [____]

b) Quality Time: [____]

c) Receiving Gifts: [____]

d) Acts of Service: [____]

e) Words of Affirmation: [____]

Your primary love language is the one with the highest score. If you have a tie, you may resonate with multiple love languages.

Discussion Space:

Discuss with your partner about your primary love language and how you both can better cater to each other's love language in daily life.

1. My primary love language is: _____

2. One thing my partner can do to cater to my love language is:

   _____

3. My partner's primary love language is: _____

4. One thing I can do to cater to my partner's love language is:

   _____

CHAPTER 3:
MASTERING THE ART OF COMMUNICATION

I n this chapter, we will delve into the realm of language, gestures, and the spaces in between. We will explore the pillars that uphold effective communication, to reduce misinterpretations and enhance empathy. As we journey further, we will also address the modern-day challenges that technology brings, from digital distractions to the nuances of texting. Armed with practical exercises and valuable insights, you will emerge better equipped to converse, connect, and truly understand your partner. Prepare to transform simple chats into meaningful conversations, building a relationship that thrives on clarity and mutual understanding.

The Foundations of Effective Communication

A midst the bustling heart of the city, two people sat across from each other in a quiet café. Their words were few, but the air was thick with unspoken emotions. The slight tilt of a head, the gentle touch of a hand, the warmth in their eyes — all these elements spoke volumes. This is the essence of communication, a dance that merges words and silences, verbal and non-verbal cues, all intertwined in a harmonious balance.

Active Listening: The bedrock of any meaningful conversation is active listening. It entails more than merely hearing words; it encompasses truly understanding the emotions and intentions behind them. It is about being present, giving your undivided attention, and displaying genuine interest in the words of the other person. By actively listening, we create a nurturing environment for open and honest communication.

Non-Verbal Cues: Often, what's left unsaid speaks louder than words. Our body language, facial expressions, and tone of voice communicate a spectrum of emotions. A reassuring touch, a comforting smile, or a concerned frown can convey feelings that words might fail to capture. Being attuned to these non-verbal cues enriches our understanding and strengthens our connection.

Tone and Timing: The way we say something holds equal significance to the content itself. A kind word spoken harshly can hurt, while a difficult truth delivered with compassion can heal. The timing of our communication is equally vital. Choosing the right moment to discuss sensitive topics ensures that both partners are receptive and open to understanding.

Practical Exercise: Spend an evening with your partner practicing active listening. One person shares a story or experience, while the other listens without interrupting. Afterward, the listener summarizes what they have heard and shares their feelings about it. This exercise helps in refining listening skills and underscores the significance of non-verbal cues.

Tip: Keep in mind that effective communication is a skill that can be nurtured. With practice, patience, and empathy, couples can master the art of genuine connection.

Surmounting Obstacles in Communication

Imagine venturing through a dense forest, where the path ahead is obscured by thick undergrowth and fallen trees. This is how communication can sometimes feel like — a journey filled with obstacles that impede our progress. Nevertheless, much like a traveler employing a machete to clear the path, couples can utilize strategies to surmount communication obstacles and establish the groundwork for meaningful conversations.

Assumptions: One of the most prevalent obstacles is making assumptions. We often presume we know what our partner is thinking or feeling, leading to misunderstandings. Rather than assuming, ask open-ended questions to gain clarity. Always remember that it is more prudent to ask and understand than to assume and misunderstand.

Emotional Reactions: Emotions can obscure our judgment and influence our responses. When emotions are running high, it becomes easy to react impulsively rather than respond thoughtfully. During such moments, take a deep breath, grant yourself a moment to process, and approach the conversation with a calm mind.

External Distractions: In today's digital age, distractions abound — from smartphones buzzing with notifications to the allure of social media. These distractions can interrupt conversations and create a sense of disconnection. Make it a practice to set aside dedicated time for meaningful conversations, free from distractions.

Practical Exercise: Engage in a "Communication Audit" with your partner. Reflect on recent conversations where communication obstacles emerged. Discuss the root causes and brainstorm strategies to surmount them in the future.

Tip: Effective communication is a two-way street. Both partners must actively participate, value listening as much as speaking, and remain open to feedback and adjustments.

The Impact of Technology on Communication

In an era where the boundaries of time and space seem to dissolve, technology stands as a beacon of innovation, reshaping the very essence of human interaction. Gone are the days when letters required weeks to traverse distances or when loved ones would eagerly await calls by the landline, hoping for a call. Today, in the blink of an eye, a message can traverse continents, bridging gaps and drawing hearts closer. The advent of smartphones, the ubiquity of social media, and the convenience of instant messaging applications have woven a digital tapestry that connects every corner of the globe. This interconnectedness, while a marvel of the modern age, is not without its intricacies. As couples navigate this digital landscape, they are presented with a unique blend of challenges and opportunities. The ease of staying connected, the delight of instant sharing, and the promise of a world accessible at one's fingertips come juxtaposed with the nuances of digital misinterpretations, the shadows of online distractions, and the gradual erosion of face-to-face intimacy. As with all revolutions, the digital age of communication necessitates a balance, a dance between the allure of the screen and the warmth of human touch.

Benefits of Digital Communication:

Constant Connectivity: Whether it is a brief text expressing love or a video call from thousands of miles away, technology ensures couples can stay connected regardless of the physical distance.

Memory Sharing: From sharing photographs of a breathtaking sunset to tagging each other in memes that induce laughter, digital platforms offer countless ways to share moments and memories.

Synchronized Activities: Watching a movie together on a streaming platform or playing an online game can be ways for couples to bond, even when they are not physically together.

Challenges of Digital Communication:

Misunderstandings: Without the nuances of tone and body language, texts and messages can easily be misinterpreted, leading to unnecessary conflicts.

Over-reliance: While technology is a valuable tool, excessive dependence on it can lead to a lack of deep, face-to-face conversations that are vital for emotional intimacy.

Distractions: The constant flood of notifications can disrupt genuine moments of connection. It is easy to prioritize a buzzing phone over a conversation with a loved one.

Strategies for Genuine Connection in a Digital Age:

Digital Detox: Allocate tech-free times, such as during meals or before bedtime, to focus entirely on one another.

Clarify Intent: If a message might be ambiguous, take a moment to seek clarification or opt for in-person discussions regarding sensitive topics.

Quality over Quantity: It is not about the frequency of messaging but the quality of conversations that matter. Make an effort to engage in meaningful conversations, even in the digital realm.

Practical Exercise: Spend an evening with your partner during which both of you set aside your devices. Engage in activities that foster connection, such as playing board games, cooking together, or simply chatting about your day.

Tip 1: Remember, technology is a tool, and it is within our control to determine how we utilize it. By being mindful and intentional, couples can harness the benefits of digital communication while preserving a genuine, profound connection.

Tip 2: Boundaries: Establish boundaries for technology use, particularly during intimate moments. For instance, avoid checking phones during date nights or deep conversations. This ensures that both partners are wholly present and engaged with one another.

Tip 3: Instead of relying solely on texts, occasionally send voice notes or video messages. Hearing a partner's voice or seeing their face can infuse a personal touch to digital interactions, making them feel more intimate and genuine.

Tip 4: Use technology to express gratitude and appreciation. Whether it involves sending a heartfelt message in the middle of the day or sharing a memory that brings a smile, small digital gestures can significantly contribute to fortifying the bond between couples.

Exercise: Communication Drills

Effective communication is the cornerstone of any strong relationship. This exercise will present you with hypothetical scenarios that couples often face. Take turns responding to each scenario, then provide feedback to your partner. Reflect on the feedback and discuss ways to improve your communication.

Instructions:

1. One partner reads a scenario aloud.
2. The other partner responds as they would in a real-life situation.
3. The reading partner provides feedback on the response.
4. Switch roles and repeat for the next scenario.
5. After all scenarios are completed, fill in the reflection prompts below.

Scenario 1: You notice that your partner has been leaving their dishes in the sink for several days.

Partner A's Response:

_____

_____

_____

Partner B's Feedback:

_____

_____

_____

Scenario 2: Your partner wants to visit their family for the holidays, but you had hoped to spend it with just the two of you.

Partner B's Response:

_____

_____

_____

Partner A's Feedback:

_____

_____

_____

Scenario 3: You both have different ideas about where to go for your next vacation. One wants a beach holiday, while the other is keen on exploring a city.

Partner A's Response:

_____

_____

_____

_____

Partner B's Feedback:

_____

_____

_____

_____

Scenario 4: Your partner forgot to pay a bill, and now you have incurred a late fee.

Partner B's Response:

_____

_____

_____

_____

Partner A's Feedback:

_____

_____

_____

_____

Reflection Prompts:

What did you learn about your partner's communication style?

_____

_____

_____

_____

How can you improve your response in a real-life situation based on the feedback received?

_____

_____

_____

_____

Were there any surprises in how your partner responded to the scenarios?

_____

_____

_____

Remember, the goal of this exercise is not to "win" the scenario but to understand each other better and improve the way you communicate. Every challenge faced together makes your bond stronger.

CHAPTER 4:

THE ESSENCE OF TRUST

In this chapter, we will look at how to develop and maintain trust so that it stands firm even in the face of life's inevitable storms. But what happens if that trust wanes? How do we repair the damage or start over? Together, we will navigate the sensitive terrain of betrayal and the pathways to recovery. Furthermore, we will touch upon the unique trust dynamics that the technological age poses in a world that is dominated by the digital realm. Explore this chapter with an open mind to learn how to create a bond that remains steadfast and true.

Establishing and Sustaining Trust

T rust in a relationship is like the roots of a tree, deeply embedded, unseen, yet crucial for holding the entire structure together. It is not built overnight but is the result of countless shared experiences, promises kept, and challenges overcome.

Consider the many instances where we place our trust in the mundane aspects of life. We trust that the chair we sit in will not collapse beneath us or that our morning coffee will be prepared to our liking. Similarly, in the realm of relationships, it is the everyday actions and gestures that serve as the foundation for trust. Punctuality for a date, attentive listening to your partner's stories, or simply being there during difficult times — these are all actions that silently convey reliability and trustworthiness.

Consistency is a pivotal factor in the process. It is not grand, infrequent gestures but steady, predictable behaviors that nurture trust. If you commit to calling at a specific time, ensure you follow through. If you make a promise to attend an event, make sure you are present. Over time, these consistent actions create a reliable pattern.

Open and honest communication is another fundamental aspect. It is crucial to maintain transparency regarding feelings, concerns, and aspirations. When partners feel they can share without fear of judgment, trust deepens. This entails establishing a safe space where both individuals can authentically express themselves.

Empathy is also of utmost importance. Taking a moment to step into your partner's shoes, understanding their perspective, and validating their emotions can significantly strengthen trust. It is not always about agreement but rather demonstrating genuine care and understanding.

Lastly, accountability plays a crucial role. We are all human, and making mistakes is inevitable. However, taking responsibility for those mistakes, acknowledging them, and taking steps to rectify them speaks volumes about one's character and trustworthiness.

Tip: Trust silently propels a relationship forward, and it should be regarded as a fragile and precious element. Once trust is broken, repairing it can be a challenging endeavor. Therefore, as you navigate the journey of love, ensure that trust remains your steadfast companion.

Rebuilding Trust Following Betrayal

Betrayal, in its multifaceted forms, can be likened to an unexpected storm that leaves devastation in its wake. Whether it manifests as infidelity, broken promises, or concealed truths, the aftermath often leaves couples grappling with shattered trust and a whirlwind of emotions. The journey to reconstruct that trust is neither straightforward nor easy, but with understanding, dedication, and time, it is achievable.

The psychology of betrayal is intricate. For the one betrayed, overwhelming feelings of hurt, anger, confusion, and self-doubt often prevail. Questions like "Why did this happen?" or "Could I have done something differently?" might haunt their thoughts. Conversely, the one responsible for the transgression may wrestle with guilt, shame, and an earnest desire to mend what has been broken.

Understanding the underlying cause of the betrayal is crucial. It is rarely about the act itself but rather rooted in deeper issues, such as unmet needs, unresolved conflicts, or personal struggles. Addressing these root causes can lay the groundwork for genuine healing.

For the healing process to begin, open communication is of paramount importance. Both parties must express their emotions, grasp each other's perspectives, and actively listen. It is not a matter of placing blame but rather fostering understanding and empathy.

Rebuilding trust necessitates unwavering effort. Small, intentional actions can yield substantial results. For the transgressor, it involves showcasing reliability, transparency, and a genuine commitment to change. For the betrayed, it is about expressing their needs, setting boundaries, and gradually allowing themselves to be vulnerable once again.

It is essential to bear in mind that trust, once broken, might never fully return to its original state. Nevertheless, this does not signify that the relationship cannot emerge stronger. Like a broken bone that heals, the bond might develop a newfound resilience, forged by the trials faced and the mutual endeavor to rebuild.

In the realm of relationships, trust is both fragile and precious. Betrayals might test their strength, but with love, understanding, and commitment, couples can navigate the stormy waters and find their way back to each other.

Trust in the Digital Age

In today's interconnected world, our relationships extend beyond face-to-face interactions. The digital realm has expanded the horizons of our connections, introducing a fresh set of challenges and opportunities regarding trust.

Social media platforms, online communities, and instant messaging applications have become integral facets of our lives. They facilitate staying in touch with loved ones, forming new friendships, and even reigniting old relationships. Nevertheless, these digital platforms also bring complexities. The ease of communication can at times blur the lines between the personal and the public, potentially leading to misunderstandings and trust-related issues. For instance, a partner might feel uneasy seeing their significant other frequently interacting with a past romantic interest on social media. Alternatively, a partner may value privacy more and feel uncomfortable with the other party sharing intimate relationship details online. These scenarios underscore the significance of establishing clear boundaries and engaging in open communication.

Setting digital boundaries is crucial. Couples should have open discussions regarding their online behaviors, comfort levels, and where they draw the line. It is imperative to respect each other's boundaries and recognize that trust in the digital age is not merely about fidelity but also about respecting privacy and comfort levels.

Moreover, trust in the digital realm also encompasses how partners support each other online. Celebrating each other's accomplishments, standing up for one another, and serving as each other's advocates on public platforms can substantially reinforce trust. However, it is also essential to remember that while digital interactions are a part of our lives, they should not replace genuine face-to-face connections. Allocating time to disconnect from the online world and investing in quality time together can help strengthen the bond and nurture trust.

Tip: In the digital age, trust involves not only fidelity but also the respect of boundaries, the appreciation of privacy, and the understanding of the intricacies of online interactions. Regularly communicate with your partner about your digital behaviors to ensure you are both on the same page.

Exercise: Trust Building Activities

Trust is the bedrock upon which a strong and enduring relationship is built. Engaging in activities designed to foster trust can significantly deepen your bond and enhance your understanding of each other. This exercise provides a list of trust-building activities that you and your partner can explore together. After each activity, take a moment to reflect on your feelings, what you learned about your partner, and how the activity influenced your trust level.

Instructions:

1. Choose an activity from the list below.
2. Engage in the activity together.
3. Reflect on the experience using the fillable sections provided.
4. Discuss your reflections with your partner.

Activity 1: Sharing a Secret - Share something with your partner that you have never told anyone else.

Your Feelings:

_____

_____

_____

What You Learned About Your Partner:

_____

_____

_____

How It Affected Your Trust Level:

_____

_____

_____

Activity 2: Discussing a Past Hurt – Talk about a time when you felt hurt in the past, whether it was in this relationship or another.

Your Feelings:

_____

_____

_____

What You Learned About Your Partner:

_____

_____

_____

How It Affected Your Trust Level:

_____

_____

_____

Activity 3: Blindfolded Guiding - One partner is blindfolded while the other guides them around the room or outdoor space, using only verbal directions.

Your Feelings:

_____

_____

_____

What You Learned About Your Partner:

_____

_____

_____

How It Affected Your Trust Level:

_____

_____

_____

Activity 4: Letter Exchange - Write a letter to your partner expressing your feelings, hopes, and dreams for the relationship. Exchange letters and read them separately. Discuss the contents afterward.

Your Feelings:

_____

_____

What You Learned About Your Partner:

_____

_____

_____

How It Affected Your Trust Level:

_____

_____

_____

Activity 5: Trust Fall - One partner stands with their back to the other and falls backward, trusting the other to catch them. Switch roles and repeat.

Your Feelings:

_____

_____

_____

What You Learned About Your Partner:

_____

_____

_____

How It Affected Your Trust Level:

_____

_____

_____

Activity 6: Memory Sharing - Sit together in a quiet space. Each partner takes a turn to share a cherished memory from their childhood or past that they have not shared before. This could be a moment of triumph, a lesson learned, or a simple, happy day. Listen intently and then discuss the feelings and emotions tied to that memory.

Your Feelings:

_____

_____

What You Learned About Your Partner:

_____

_____

How It Affected Your Trust Level:

_____

_____

Remember, trust is built over time and through consistent actions. These activities are just a starting point. Continue to nurture trust in your relationship through open communication, mutual understanding, and love.

CHAPTER 5:

ADDRESSING INFIDELITY AND BETRAYAL

Infidelity and betrayal are among the difficult things a couple can go through. This chapter probes the core of these traumatic experiences, seeking understanding and ways for healing. Instead of only concentrating on the act, we will delve further into the cause of infidelity, providing a more fundamental understanding of why it occurs. This chapter offers advice on how couples can emerge stronger, wiser, and more connected, despite the potential for severe emotional scarring. We will also touch upon the psychological effects of betrayal, ensuring you and your partner have a holistic understanding. Through reflective exercises and insights, this chapter serves as a beacon of hope, illuminating the path to healing and renewed trust.

Understanding the Causes of Infidelity

Infidelity presents a complex issue, often veiled in pain, confusion, and a multitude of emotions. While it is easy to label the act as a mere betrayal, understanding its underlying causes can offer clarity and pave the way for healing. So, what drives someone to stray from a committed relationship?

Influence of Society: We live in a world that often celebrates instant gratification. The allure of the 'new' and the 'exciting' is constantly paraded in media, subtly suggesting that novelty might be more satisfying than the familiar. This societal norm can sometimes seep into our personal lives, making some believe that a new relationship or a fleeting affair might offer the happiness they seek.

Emotional Void: At times, individuals may sense emotional distance or disconnection from their partners. This emotional void can drive them to seek validation, understanding, or intimacy elsewhere. It is not always about physical attraction; sometimes, the yearning for an emotional connection leads to infidelity.

Personal Struggles: Personal insecurities, past traumas, or unresolved personal issues can also play a role. Someone battling low self-esteem might seek external validation through multiple relationships. Or an experience might have instilled the belief that they do not deserve a stable, loving relationship.

The Thrill of the Forbidden: For some, the very act of doing something forbidden provides a thrill. The secrecy, the risk of being discovered, and the allure of the unknown can be intoxicating for some individuals.

External Pressures: Sometimes, external factors like work-related stress, peer pressure, or significant life changes can compel individuals to make choices they might not have considered otherwise.

Tip: While understanding the reasons behind infidelity can provide clarity, it is crucial to remember that reasons are not excuses. Open communication, seeking professional guidance, and addressing underlying issues are vital steps for couples aiming to rebuild trust and move forward.

Healing and Moving Forward

The aftermath of infidelity can be a turbulent period for couples, marked by a whirlwind of emotions, doubts, and questions. The path to recovery is neither linear nor easy, but with commitment, understanding, and effort, it is possible to rebuild the trust that was broken.

The Power of Forgiveness: Forgiveness is not about condoning the act but rather about liberating oneself from the shackles of resentment and anger. It is a personal journey that allows the betrayed partner to find peace and move forward. However, forgiveness does not mean forgetting; it means choosing to heal and grow from the experience.

Seeking Professional Help: Therapy can be a valuable tool in the healing process. A trained therapist can create a safe environment for both partners to express their feelings, understand the underlying causes of the infidelity, and develop strategies to rebuild trust. Couples therapy, in particular, can offer insights into the dynamics of the relationship and guide couples toward a healthier future.

Recommitting to Each Other: After an act of infidelity, both partners must recommit to the relationship. This might involve renewing vows, setting new relationship goals, or simply spending quality time together to rekindle the bond.

Rebuilding Trust: Trust, once broken, takes time to rebuild. It requires consistent effort, transparency, and commitment from both partners. Setting boundaries, spending quality time together, and reaffirming commitment can help in regaining lost trust.

Tip: Set aside regular "check-in" moments with your partner, perhaps during a weekly date night or a quiet evening at home. Use this time to discuss feelings, progress, and any concerns related to trust. This consistent effort can help both partners feel connected and understood as they navigate the healing process.

The Psychological Impact of Betrayal

Betrayal, especially in the context of a romantic relationship, can inflict profound emotional wounds. The psychological impact of such an act can be substantial, affecting both the person who was betrayed and the one who committed the betrayal. Let us explore the emotional landscape of betrayal and the paths to healing.

For the betrayed, the revelation of infidelity can resemble the sudden removal of solid ground beneath their feet. Trust, once a given, now becomes a question mark. Emotions such as anger, sadness, confusion, and even self-doubt may inundate them. Questions like "Was it something I did?" or "Why was I not enough?" might occupy their thoughts. The emotional toll can also manifest in physical symptoms, such as disruptions in sleep, changes in appetite, or even anxiety and depression.

On the other hand, the one who committed the act of betrayal might grapple with guilt, shame, and regret. They might fear losing the relationship and the love they once took for granted. The weight of their actions and the pain they have caused can be overwhelming.

Coping mechanisms become essential during this period. For the betrayed, seeking support from trusted friends, family, or therapists can be invaluable. Expressing emotions, rather than bottling them up, can aid in the healing process. For the one who strays, taking responsibility for their actions, seeking therapy, and genuinely striving for atonement can pave the way for personal growth and understanding.

The journey of emotional healing is lengthy and varies for each person. Some couples might find a way back to each other, rebuilding their relationship stronger than before. Others might choose separate paths, seeking peace and growth individually. Regardless of the outcome, understanding the psychological impact of betrayal is the first step toward healing.

Tip: If you find yourself ruminating on the betrayal, set aside a specific time each day to process these feelings. This designated "emotional processing time" can help compartmentalize the pain, enabling you to function in daily life without being constantly overwhelmed.

Exercise: Path to Healing

Betrayal, regardless of its manifestation, has the potential to inflict profound emotional wounds. The resulting pain can be utterly overwhelming, whether it takes the form of infidelity, broken promises, or hidden truths. It is crucial to grasp and work through these emotions as a fundamental step toward the journey of healing.

Current Emotional State: *What emotions are you currently feeling?*

_____

_____

_____

_____

Understanding the Root Cause: *Reflect on the event or series of events that led to the betrayal. Can you identify the root cause or underlying issues?*

_____

_____

_____

_____

Needs for Healing: *What do you need from your partner to heal?*

_____

_____

_____

_____

Commitment to Rebuilding Trust: *What can you both commit to in order to rebuild trust?*

_____

_____

_____

_____

Personal Reflection: *How has this betrayal changed your perspective on trust and relationships?*

_____

_____

_____

_____

Steps Forward: *List down three actionable steps you both can take in the coming weeks to start the healing process.*

_____

_____

_____

_____

Remember, healing is a journey. It requires patience, understanding, and consistent effort from both partners. Use this exercise as a starting point to open up a dialogue and work toward a stronger, more trusting relationship.

CHAPTER 6:
EMOTIONAL INTIMACY AND DEEP CONNECTION

The realm of emotional intimacy, where souls intertwine and genuine connections are established, goes beyond the passionate embraces and whispered sweet nothings. The emotional bonds that anchor and sustain a relationship are explored in this chapter along with other less obvious but no less significant aspects of relationships. We will peel back the curtain on emotional intimacy so you can understand its depth and importance. You will be better able to support and strengthen the emotional bonds with your partner if you understand how shared experiences and moments of vulnerability develop this deep connection. Dive in and learn how to forge connections that go past the surface and to the very heart of your shared journey.

The Layers of Emotional Intimacy

E motional intimacy is often likened to peeling back the layers of an onion. Each layer represents a deeper level of connection, understanding, and vulnerability. But what exactly does it mean to be emotionally intimate with someone, and why is it pivotal in a relationship? At its essence, emotional intimacy revolves around truly understanding and being understood by another person. It entails feeling secure enough to share your deepest fears, hopes, dreams, and insecurities with someone, knowing that judgment or dismissal is not on the horizon.

Surface-Level Interactions: Being the outermost layer of emotional intimacy, this encompasses casual conversations about daily events, such as discussing the weather or recounting the day's events. Though seemingly trivial, these interactions lay the groundwork for more profound connections.

Shared Experiences: As you peel back the layers, you find shared experiences. These are the memories you create together, from vacations to personal milestones. They serve as a bond, reminding both partners of their shared journey and the moments that have shaped their relationship.

Emotional Sharing: Delving further, we come to emotional sharing. This is where you begin to open up about your feelings, fears, and dreams. It is a vulnerable space, but it is also where true connection starts to form.

Deep Vulnerability: The innermost layer of emotional intimacy is deep vulnerability. Not only joys but also insecurities, past traumas, and profound fears are shared. It is the space where one reveals their true self, imperfections and all, trusting that their partner will honor and cherish that vulnerability.

Emotional intimacy is the glue that holds relationships together. It is what differentiates a deep, meaningful relationship from a superficial one. By understanding and nurturing each layer, couples can forge a bond that stands the test of time, challenges, and life's unpredictable twists and turns.

Tip: To nurture emotional intimacy, set aside regular "heart-to-heart" sessions with your partner. Use this time to discuss not just the events of the day but also your feelings, dreams, and fears. It is a simple yet powerful way to deepen your connection.

Cultivating Deep Connection

Fostering a deep connection goes beyond merely understanding each other's emotions. It involves actively nurturing and fostering that bond, ensuring it grows stronger with time. Here is how couples can cultivate and deepen their emotional connection:

Active Listening: A powerful tool for fostering connection is the art of active listening. It is not just about hearing the words but understanding the emotions and sentiments behind them. Giving undivided attention when your partner speaks demonstrates that you value their thoughts and feelings, fostering a deeper bond.

Quality Time: In today's fast-paced world, spending quality time together can often take a backseat. However, it is these moments, free from distractions, that can significantly deepen your connection. Whether it is a regular date night, a walk in the park, or just cooking together, these shared moments are priceless.

Openness and Honesty: Being open and honest about your feelings, even when it is challenging, can significantly deepen trust and intimacy. It involves revealing your true self, with all its imperfections, and trusting that your partner will embrace it.

Mutual Growth: As individuals, we are continually growing and evolving. Supporting each other's personal growth journeys ensures that couples grow together, not apart. Whether it is attending workshops, reading books, or exploring new hobbies together, mutual growth can be a bonding experience.

Physical Intimacy: While emotional intimacy is crucial, physical intimacy also plays a vital role in deepening connection. It is not just about the act itself but the closeness, warmth, and comfort that accompany it. From holding hands to cuddling on the couch, these moments of physical connection complement and enhance emotional intimacy.

Tip: Start a gratitude journal together. Each day, jot down one thing you are grateful for about your partner or your relationship. Sharing these moments of gratitude can foster appreciation and deepen your connection.

The Significance of Shared Experiences

Shared experiences are the threads that weave the fabric of a relationship. They are the moments that define us, the memories we cherish, and the stories we tell. But why are they so crucial in deepening emotional intimacy?

Creating Bonds: When you share an experience, whether it is as simple as watching a movie together or as grand as traveling to a new country, you are creating a bond. It is a moment that is exclusive to just the two of you, a memory that you will always share.

Building Trust: Facing challenges and navigating new experiences together can strengthen trust. Whether it is getting lost in a new city or facing a personal challenge, working through these situations together can solidify your bond.

Understanding Each Other: Shared experiences provide insights into each other's personalities, fears, dreams, and quirks. You get to see how your partner reacts in different situations, giving you a deeper understanding of who they are.

Creating Joy: The joy of experiencing something new or revisiting cherished memories can reignite passion and happiness in a relationship. It is a reminder of why you fell in love and the adventures you have shared.

Growth as a Couple: Every experience, whether good or bad, offers a lesson. By reflecting on these shared moments, couples can grow together, understanding what works for them and what they would like to avoid in the future.

So, how can couples intentionally create meaningful experiences together?

Plan Regular Date Nights: It does not have to be extravagant. The key is to spend quality time together, away from the distractions of daily life.

Travel Together: Exploring new places can be a bonding experience. It does not have to be an international trip; even a weekend getaway can offer fresh perspectives.

Learn Together: Take up a new hobby or class. Whether it is dancing, cooking, or a language class, learning something new can be both fun and bonding.

Celebrate Milestones: Whether it is an anniversary, a promotion, or a personal achievement, celebrate it. It is a reminder of your journey together.

Revisit Old Memories: Sometimes, revisiting places from your past, like where you first met or had your first date, can reignite those initial feelings of love and excitement.

Engage in Acts of Service: Doing something kind for your partner, be it preparing a surprise meal or taking over a chore they dislike, can create cherished memories. These acts show thoughtfulness and care.

Attend Workshops or Retreats: Participating in couples' workshops or retreats can be a transformative experience. It offers a chance to deepen understanding, learn new relationship skills, and connect on a deeper level.

Cultural Experiences: Attend cultural events or festivals together. Experiencing different cultures can broaden your horizons and give you fresh topics to discuss.

Nature Escapes: Spend a day outdoors, be it hiking, picnicking, or just watching the sunset. Nature has a way of calming the mind and allowing for deeper connections.

Home Projects: Take up a home project together, like gardening, redecorating a room, or even DIY crafts. Working toward a common goal can be bonding.

Book Club for Two: Choose a book to read together. Discussing the plot, characters, and themes can lead to deeper conversations about personal beliefs and values.

Cooking Challenges: Pick a cuisine or dish you both have not tried before and cook it together. The process, from shopping for ingredients to tasting the final dish, can be a fun and rewarding experience.

Stargazing: Spend a night under the stars. It is a humbling experience that can lead to profound conversations and a deeper appreciation for the universe and each other.

Tip: Create a "memory jar." Whenever you share a special moment or experience, jot it down on a piece of paper and place it in the jar. On anniversaries or whenever you feel like reminiscing, open the jar and relive those memories.

Exercise: Deep Dive Discussions

Building a deep emotional connection requires more than just surface-level conversations. It is about diving deep, exploring vulnerabilities, and truly understanding each other's dreams, fears, and aspirations. Use the following conversation starters to foster a profound connection with your partner. After discussing each prompt, take a moment to write down your thoughts and reflections.

True Understanding: *Describe a time you felt truly seen and understood.*

Partner A:

_____

_____

_____

Partner B:

_____

_____

_____

Hidden Dreams: *What is a dream you have never shared with anyone?*

Partner A:

_____

_____

_____

Partner B:

_____

_____

_____

Vulnerable Moments: *Share a moment when you felt most vulnerable. How did it shape you?*

Partner A:

_____

_____

_____

Partner B:

_____

_____

_____

Childhood Memories: *Which childhood memory has had the most significant impact on who you are today?*

Partner A:

_____

_____

_____

Partner B:

_____

_____

_____

Personal Growth: _Describe a challenge you overcame and how it contributed to your personal growth._

Partner A:

_____

_____

_____

Partner B:

_____

_____

_____

Future Aspirations: _Where do you see yourself in ten years, and what role does our relationship play in that vision?_

Partner A:

_____

_____

_____

Partner B:

_____

_____

_____

Core Values: *What are the three core values that guide your life, and why are they important to you?*

Partner A:

_____

_____

_____

Partner B:

_____

_____

_____

Engaging in these deep-dive discussions will not only strengthen your bond but also provide insights into each other's worlds. Remember, the journey of understanding is ongoing. Revisit these prompts periodically to see how your answers evolve.

CHAPTER 7:

KEEPING THE PASSION ALIVE THROUGH PHYSICAL INTIMACY

In this chapter, we explore the world of physical closeness and its ability to transform a partnership. We will examine how crucial it is to maintain love, particularly as relationships change over time. However, the focus extends beyond fiery passion; we will also address the challenges and external factors that can influence this intimate connection. Through engaging exercises and insightful discussions, you will be guided toward rekindling the spark and ensuring the flames of passion burn bright, regardless of the years or challenges you face together. Approach this chapter with an open heart and mind, ready to celebrate and nurture the physical bond you share.

The Role of Physical Intimacy

In the early stages of a relationship, the mere touch of a partner's hand or a tender embrace can send shivers down one's spine. The thrill of a first kiss, the warmth of a hug, or the comfort of a cuddle on a cold night—these are moments that many cherish. However, physical intimacy transcends mere passionate encounters; it represents a deeper, more profound connection that extends beyond the physical realm.

Physical intimacy is a language of its own. It is a way of communicating love, trust, and a sense of belonging. It encompasses more than just sexual interactions, emphasizing the importance of simple touches, moments of closeness, and gestures that convey the reassuring message, "I am here for you."

The Psychological Benefits of Touch

From a psychological standpoint, touch fulfills a fundamental human need. Studies have shown that babies who are deprived of touch can suffer from developmental and emotional issues later in life. Touch triggers the release of oxytocin, often referred to as the "love hormone." This hormone plays a crucial role in bonding and increases feelings of trust and connection between individuals.

Moreover, touch can be a source of comfort. Think about the times you have felt down, stressed, or anxious. A comforting touch from a loved one made you feel better, right? That is because touch can reduce levels of the stress hormone cortisol, promoting relaxation and a sense of ease.

Emotional Depth Through Physical Closeness

Physical intimacy emerges as a key player in deepening emotional connections between partners. In moments of physical closeness, couples are not merely sharing their bodies; they are sharing their hearts and souls. These moments allow for a level of connection that transcends the limitations of verbal communication.

For instance, after a disagreement, a simple act of holding hands can bridge the gap of words left unsaid. A hug can melt away fears, and a kiss can heal wounds of the heart. These acts of physical intimacy become anchors in a relationship, reminding couples of their love and commitment to each other.

Beyond the Physical: A Deeper Connection

While the physical facets of intimacy are essential, they are just one piece of the puzzle. True intimacy is about understanding, trust, and emotional connection. It involves being vulnerable, allowing someone to see the real you, and accepting them for who they are.

Physical intimacy is a celebration of this deeper emotional bond. It is a means of expressing love, trust, and commitment without uttering a word. It is a reminder that in the vastness of this world, two people have chosen to be close, to share their lives, their joys, their sorrows, and their dreams.

Tip 1: Physical intimacy is not just about grand gestures. Sometimes, the most profound connections are made through simple acts. A surprise hug from behind while cooking, holding hands during a movie, or a gentle touch on the face can speak volumes. Prioritize these small moments of closeness; they are the building blocks of a deep, lasting connection.

Tip 2: Make it a habit to greet each other with a hug or a kiss when you meet after a long day. These routine gestures can become cherished moments that you both look forward to.

Tip 3: Set aside time once a week or even once a month for a massage exchange. It does not have to be professional; the act itself fosters intimacy and relaxation.

Tip 4: Sometimes, intimacy is not just about touch. Holding deep, meaningful eye contact for a few moments can create a profound connection without a word spoken.

Tip 5: Even if you are not a dancer, swaying to a favorite song in your living room can be a fun and intimate experience.

Tip 6: Whether it is a gentle squeeze on the arm, a pat on the back, or a playful tickle, these spontaneous touches can keep the spark alive.

Tip 7: Even when going to bed, a simple act like spooning or holding hands can foster a sense of closeness and security.

Evolving Passion in Long-Term Relationships

In the honeymoon phase of a relationship, passion feels effortless, driven by novelty and discovery. But as relationships mature, this spontaneous fervor transitions to a deeper, more intentional connection. It is not about the fiery start but the profound bond that develops over time.

Rediscovering Each Other: Even in the most familiar relationships, there is always something new to discover. As individuals evolve, so do their dreams, fears, and aspirations. Setting aside time to delve into these deeper conversations can reignite the sense of discovery that characterized the relationship's early days. It is a reminder that there is always more to learn, and more to explore, even in the most familiar terrains.

Shared Rituals: Routine can be both comforting and monotonous. To break the monotony, consider establishing shared rituals. It could be a weekly cooking session where both experiment with a new recipe, or perhaps a monthly "unplugged" day where digital devices are set aside in favor of board games, books, or nature walks. These rituals become more than just activities; they are shared moments of connection, fostering intimacy and understanding.

Embracing Vulnerability: While physical intimacy is often celebrated, emotional vulnerability is the bedrock of deep connections. Letting your guard down, and sharing your deepest insecurities, hopes, and memories can foster an intimacy that is profound and enduring. It is in these moments of raw honesty that couples truly connect.

Challenges as Catalysts: Every relationship faces its share of storms. However, when faced together, these challenges can serve as catalysts for a deeper connection.

Tip: Dedicate an hour each week as "our time," free from distractions and external commitments. Just two people reconnecting. Whether it is through conversation, shared activities, or simply sitting in silence, this dedicated time can serve as a powerful reminder of the bond shared.

The Influence of External Factors on Physical Intimacy

Life is a series of ebbs and flows, and just as the tides of the ocean are influenced by external forces, so too is our physical intimacy. External factors, often beyond our control, can significantly influence the dynamics of romantic relationships. Health concerns, mounting work stress, and major life changes can all cast a shadow over the bedroom, making physical connection seem like a distant memory.

Take, for instance, the story of Sarah and Mark, a couple in their mid-30s. While they once enjoyed a vibrant physical relationship, recent changes have shifted the dynamic. Sarah's diagnosis of a medical condition affecting her energy levels and libido coincided with Mark's increasing work pressure. Their once passionate nights have now turned into silent evenings of watching TV and going to bed early.

It is not uncommon for couples to experience such phases. Health issues, whether they are temporary like a bout of flu, or more long-term, can significantly impact one's desire and ability to be physically intimate. Medications, treatments, and the emotional toll of a diagnosis can all play a part.

Work stress is another common factor. Long hours, demanding bosses, and the constant pressure to perform can leave individuals drained, both mentally and physically. When you are mentally preoccupied, it becomes challenging to be present in intimate moments, leading to a disconnect.

Life changes, such as the birth of a child, moving to a new city, or even the loss of a loved one, can also shift the dynamics of physical intimacy. These events, while natural, require adjustment and can temporarily divert attention from the couple's physical relationship.

However, all is not lost. Awareness is the first step toward navigating these challenges. Couples can take proactive measures by recognizing the external factors affecting their intimacy. Open communication is crucial, and seeking professional guidance, such as couples therapy, can provide tools and strategies to reignite physical connection.

In conclusion, while external factors are a part of life, they do not have to define a relationship. With understanding, patience, and effort, couples can navigate these challenges and maintain a deep and meaningful physical connection.

Exercise: Intimacy Challenge

Physical intimacy extends beyond the realm of a mere physical act; it serves as a profound means to emotionally connect with your partner. This challenge is designed to help you explore and deepen that connection. As you go through each activity, take a moment to reflect on the emotions it elicits and the insights it offers about your relationship.

Eye Gazing: Sit across from each other, and maintain eye contact for three minutes without speaking.

Reflection: How did maintaining eye contact make you feel? Did any emotions or memories surface?

Partner A:

_____

_____

_____

Partner B:

_____

_____

_____

Hold Each Other: Embrace each other for five uninterrupted minutes. Focus on the warmth, the heartbeat, and the comfort.

Reflection: What emotions did you feel during the embrace? Did it bring back any memories or create new ones?

Partner A:

_____

_____

_____

Partner B:

_____

_____

_____

Dance Together: Choose a song, any song, and dance together. It does not matter if it is slow or fast, just move together.

Reflection: How did dancing together make you feel? Did it remind you of any past moments or inspire future ones?

Partner A:

_____

_____

_____

Partner B:

_____

_____

_____

Hand Massage: Take turns giving each other a five-minute hand massage. Use gentle pressure and focus on the touch.

Reflection: How did the touch of your partner's hands make you feel? What did you learn about the power of touch?

Partner A:

_____

_____

_____

Partner B:

_____

_____

_____

Whispered Words: Whisper something you have never told your partner before. It can be a secret, a memory, or a dream.

Reflection: How did it feel to share and listen to something so intimate in such a close setting?

Partner A:

_____

_____

_____

Partner B:

_____

_____

_____

CHAPTER 8:

THE DANCE BETWEEN PERSONAL AND SHARED GROWTH

This chapter shines a light on how to nurture individual passions and dreams while maintaining a delicate balance with the shared aspirations of the relationship. Through interactive exercises and insightful reflections, discover a roadmap for harmonizing the dance between personal evolution and shared progression. Embark on this exploration to unlock the full potential of a relationship that fosters growth both individually and together.

The Journey of Individual Growth

In every relationship, two distinct personalities embark on unique journeys of personal growth. Love binds them, but their journeys add depth, character, and resilience to the relationship.

Prioritizing personal growth strengthens the relationship, like two trees whose roots intertwine, growing stronger together while reaching for individual heights.

Emotional, intellectual, or spiritual, profoundly impact the dynamics of a relationship. As individuals evolve, fresh perspectives, deeper understanding, and renewed energy enrich shared lives, ensuring adaptability to life's changes and challenges with grace and resilience.

However, personal growth is not just about attending workshops or setting career milestones. It is about introspection, acknowledging our imperfections, and working toward bettering ourselves. It is about setting personal goals, be they related to hobbies, health, or personal well-being, and pursuing them with passion.

In this journey, a partner's support is crucial in celebrating successes, offering solace during setbacks, and understanding when solitude is needed.

In the grand tapestry of a relationship, individual growth threads run parallel to shared experiences, sometimes intertwining, sometimes running independently, but always adding to the richness of the shared life.

Tip: Dedicate time for "relationship reflections" to discuss individual growth experiences, achievements, and aspirations. This practice not only fosters mutual understanding but also ensures that both partners are in sync in their shared journey.

The Power of Shared Growth

While personal growth is vital, there is unparalleled magic in growing together as a couple. Shared growth involves harnessing the collective energy of two souls, working toward common goals, and evolving together.

Imagine a garden where two plants grow side by side. If they are nurtured individually, they will grow, no doubt. But if they are given the chance to intertwine, to share the same soil, sunlight, and water, they not only grow but flourish together, supporting each other during storms and basking in the sun's glow together. This is the essence of shared growth in a relationship.

Shared experiences, be it traveling to a new place, learning a new skill, or even overcoming a challenge, create memories that last a lifetime. These experiences become stories that couples recount, laugh over, and sometimes even cry about. They become the foundation upon which trust is built and love is deepened.

Setting shared goals is another powerful way to foster growth. It could be as simple as saving up for a dream vacation, adopting a healthier lifestyle, or as profound as supporting each other's career aspirations. When couples work toward a common goal, they learn to compromise, adjust, and most importantly, celebrate each other's successes as their own.

Challenges, though often seen as hurdles, can be catalysts for shared growth. Facing financial hardships, dealing with health issues, or navigating the complexities of family dynamics can be tough. But when faced together, these challenges become opportunities to understand, support, and stand by each other. They teach resilience, patience, and the true meaning of partnership.

In the end, shared growth is about creating a life narrative that is co-authored. It is about celebrating the joys, facing the storms, and cherishing the calm together. It is about understanding that while individual growth is about "me," shared growth is about "us." And in this journey of "us," lies the true power of a relationship.

The Role of External Support Systems

Even the strongest couples may require guidance or a listening ear from outside their partnership. This is where external support systems come into play, acting as a safety net and offering fresh perspectives. These systems, whether they be friends, family, or professional therapists, can provide invaluable insights and advice that can help couples navigate the complexities of their relationship.

Friends and family, having witnessed individuals at their best and worst, provide unique insights and serve as a sounding board, offering a safe space to vent, seek advice, or simply be heard. They can remind couples of their individual strengths and how they have successfully overcome past challenges.

However, while friends and family are invaluable, there are times when professional guidance is necessary. Therapists or counselors are trained to help couples navigate relationship challenges, offering tools and strategies tailored to each couple's unique situation. They provide an objective viewpoint, free from personal biases or past experiences. Engaging in couples therapy does not signify failure; instead, it shows a commitment to growth and a willingness to seek help when needed.

Beyond therapy, joining support groups or attending relationship workshops can also be beneficial. These settings allow couples to learn from others who might be facing similar challenges, fostering a sense of community and shared understanding.

Incorporating external support does not mean a couple is incapable of resolving issues on their own. Instead, it is a recognition that growth is a journey, and sometimes, we all need a little help along the way. By leaning on these support systems, couples can gain new insights, learn effective communication strategies, and strengthen their bond.

Tip: When seeking advice, filter feedback, prioritizing the unique dynamics of your relationship. What works for one couple may not work for another, and integrating external advice should align with your partnership's needs and values.

Exercise: Growth Map

Individual Growth Goals: Personal growth is about evolving into the best version of yourself. It is about learning, adapting, and striving for a better tomorrow. Setting individual growth goals will not only benefit you but will also enrich your relationship.

Learning a New Skill

Goal:

Steps to Achieve:

_____

_____

_____

Reflection: How will acquiring this skill benefit you and your relationship?

_____

_____

_____

Personal Wellness

Goal:

Steps to Achieve:

_____

_____

_____

Reflection: How will focusing on this wellness goal impact your well-being and the health of your relationship?

_____

_____

_____

Shared Growth Goals: Shared growth goals are about evolving together as a unit. It is about creating memories, facing challenges, and celebrating victories together.

Traveling Together

Destination:

Reason for Choosing:

_____

_____

Steps to Prepare:

_____

_____

Reflection: What do you hope to experience and learn from this journey together?

_____

_____

Attending a Workshop or Class

Workshop/Class Name:

Reason for Choosing:

_____

_____

_____

Steps to Prepare:

_____

_____

_____

Reflection: How do you think this shared experience will strengthen your bond?

_____

_____

_____

Monthly Check-in: Set aside time each month to revisit your Growth Map. Discuss the progress you have made, the challenges you have faced, and the adjustments you might need to make to your goals.

What progress have we made toward our individual and shared growth goals?

_____

_____

_____

How have we supported each other's growth journey this month?

_____

_____

_____

_____

_____

What adjustments, if any, do we need to make to our Growth Map?

_____

_____

_____

_____

_____

Remember, growth is a continuous journey. Celebrate your milestones, no matter how small, and always strive to be better together.

CHAPTER 9:

THE SIGNIFICANCE OF HOBBIES AND SHARED INTERESTS

In this chapter, we delve into the significance of hobbies and shared experiences, recognizing them as more than mere pastimes. They are the threads weaving moments of joy, understanding, and connection within a relationship. Explore the exhilarating world of shared experiences and learn how they can fortify bonds and deepen understanding between partners. While celebrating shared interests, we equally emphasize the importance of respecting and navigating differences that contribute to the uniqueness of each partner. This exploration provides insights into striking a harmonious balance between shared endeavors and individual passions, ensuring a relationship that celebrates both togetherness and individuality. Through engaging exercises and thoughtful discussions, you will be equipped to design moments that enhance connection, understanding, and mutual appreciation. Embark on this journey and discover the joy inherent in both shared and individual pursuits of love.

The Bonding Power of Shared Activities

Picture entering a dance studio for the first time alongside your significant other. The air resonates with the gentle strumming of a Spanish guitar, and the instructor guides you through a basic salsa step. Together, you stumble, occasionally stepping on each other's toes, and share hearty laughter. By the session's end, not only have you acquired a few dance moves, but you have also uncovered a new facet of your partner, deepening your connection.

Engaging in shared activities, whether it is dancing, hiking, painting, or cooking, presents couples with a distinctive chance to strengthen their bond. It transcends the activity itself, encompassing a journey of exploration, understanding, and mutual growth.

Venturing into new hobbies or pursuits with your partner means stepping out of your comfort zones collectively. This shared vulnerability acts as a potent bonding agent, especially in moments of uncertainty — like attempting to pitch a tent for the first time or mastering the art of kneading dough — where you become each other's cheerleader, teacher, and student all at once. Furthermore, shared activities provide a respite from the daily grind. Amid the hustle and bustle of routine, it is easy to slip into predictability and take one another for granted. Yet, when immersed in learning pottery or attending a photography class together, you see your partner through fresh eyes. The qualities that initially attracted you resurface, reigniting a sense of discovery.

But it is not just about novelty. Engaging in shared activities creates a reservoir of memories. These memories become stories you tell, experiences you look back on, and most importantly, they serve as a reminder of the bond you share. In the journey of love and companionship, while individual growth is paramount, the moments you grow together are equally precious. So, the next time you come across an interesting workshop or a new trail, consider inviting your partner. It might just be the adventure you both need.

Tip: Start small and simple. If you are unsure about which activity to pick up together, begin with something that requires minimal investment and preparation. It could be as straightforward as trying out a new recipe together or taking evening walks in a nearby park. The key is consistency and enjoying the process together.

Harmonizing Differences in Interests

Within every relationship, individuals bring a unique array of interests, hobbies, and passions. While engaging in shared activities can foster connection, it is entirely natural for couples to possess distinct interests. These differences, if not understood and respected, might lead to tension. However, when approached with consideration, these differences can become sources of strength and growth for the relationship. Consider the case of Sarah and Alex — Sarah immerses herself in novels for hours, finding solace in her reading nook, while Alex is fervently passionate about mountain biking, seeking thrill on the trails. Initially, understanding each other's preferences posed a challenge. Sarah could not grasp the appeal of strenuous uphill biking, and Alex could not comprehend spending hours engrossed in a book. Yet, over time, they learned to navigate these differences. Here is how they, and many couples like them, manage to balance individual interests with shared growth:

Respect Each Other's Passions: It is crucial to acknowledge the value inherent in each person's hobby or interest, even if it does not align with your own. Genuine respect for your partner's passions establishes an environment of mutual respect.
Find the Overlap: While the core activities may differ, underlying emotions or experiences can often be similar. Sarah found escapism in her books, mirroring the thrill Alex experienced biking through nature. They began sharing their experiences — Sarah discussing her latest book plot and Alex describing his recent trail adventure.
Try It Out: Occasionally, step into your partner's world. Sarah accompanied Alex on a beginner's biking trail, and Alex spent an afternoon reading alongside Sarah. While they did not fully adopt each other's hobbies, they gained a deeper appreciation for them.
Create 'Us' Time: While pursuing individual interests is healthy, it is also crucial to carve out activities that both partners enjoy. It could be something as simple as a weekly movie night or attending a pottery class together.
Communicate: If you ever sense that individual hobbies are consuming too much time, communicate your feelings. Finding a balance ensures both personal growth and the nurturing of the relationship.

In navigating these differences, couples can cultivate an environment where individual passions coexist harmoniously with shared experiences, fostering a relationship that thrives on both individuality and togetherness.

The Balance of Individuality and Togetherness

Within every relationship, there exists a nuanced dance between individuality and togetherness. Envision two artists collaborating on the same canvas — each contributes unique colors and strokes, yet they strive to create a harmonious masterpiece together. Likewise, in relationships, both partners bring their passions, interests, and hobbies. While shared activities strengthen the bond, individual pursuits introduce depth and dimension to the relationship.

Have you observed the sparkle in your partner's eyes when they recount a solo hiking trip or discuss their experiences in a pottery class? These individual escapades not only contribute to personal growth but also infuse a sense of freshness and novelty into the relationship. Engaging in separate hobbies allows partners to gather new stories, experiences, and insights to later share, fostering excitement and curiosity as each gets a glimpse into the other's world.

Furthermore, individual hobbies provide a haven for self-reflection, relaxation, and rejuvenation — a time to connect with oneself, free from the roles and responsibilities of the relationship. When partners return to the relationship after such breaks, they often bring renewed energy and perspective.

However, it is equally vital to discover shared activities that both partners enjoy. These shared experiences become threads weaving a tighter relationship fabric, creating memories, fostering deeper understanding, and building a shared history. Whether it involves attending a dance class, cooking together, or volunteering for a cause, these activities solidify the connection.

Navigating this delicate balance requires effective communication and an understanding of each other's needs. While supporting individual pursuits is essential, finding time for shared activities is equally vital. Regular check-ins, discussions, and planning ensure that both individuality and togetherness rightfully coexist within the relationship.

In the end, it is about understanding that while two people come together to share a life, they remain two distinct individuals. Celebrating this individuality while cherishing the shared moments is the key to a fulfilling relationship. Remember, it is not about losing oneself in the relationship but about growing together while also nurturing one's essence.

Exercise: Shared Activity Planner

Participating in shared activities is a powerful way to strengthen the connection between partners. This not only facilitates the creation of lasting memories but also contributes to a profound understanding of each other's interests, passions, and quirks. This exercise is crafted to guide you in exploring fresh hobbies and activities as a couple, nurturing a deeper connection and mutual understanding.

Activity Exploration List: List down hobbies or activities you both have expressed interest in or are curious about. This will serve as your go-to list when planning shared activities.

Activity Name	Who Suggested?	Date to Try

Activity Reflection: After trying out each activity, take a moment to reflect on the experience. This will help you understand what you both enjoyed and what you might want to explore further.

Briefly describe the activity and what it entailed.

_____

_____

What did you enjoy most about the activity?

_____

_____

Did you learn something new about your partner or yourself during this activity?

_____

_____

Would you like to continue this activity together in the future? (Yes/No)

Monthly Activity Check-in: It is essential to regularly revisit your activity list and reflections. This will help you plan future activities and understand the patterns of what you both enjoy the most.

Which activities have we tried this month and what have we learned from them?

_____

_____

_____

_____

Are there any activities we would like to try again or explore further?

_____

_____

What new activities can we add to our exploration list for the coming month?

_____

_____

Remember, the goal is not just to do activities together but to understand, connect, and grow closer through shared experiences. Enjoy the journey of discovery!

Fostering Stronger Relationships Together

For many couples, navigating the complexities of their relationship can sometimes feel like navigating through a dense forest without a compass. The whirlwind of emotions, past experiences, and daily challenges can make it hard to see the bigger picture. That overwhelming sensation where love and frustration coexist, where passion meets daily grind, is something all couples encounter at some point.

When I set out to write this book, my vision was not only to provide you with tools and exercises to build a better bond with your partner but also to remind you that every relationship has its ups and downs. That you are not alone in your quest to find mutual understanding, trust, and intimacy.

So, here is a small invitation for you, and it is an opportunity that goes beyond just you and your partner. You have the chance to let countless other couples know they are not wandering alone in that vast relationship forest. How, you ask? Simply by sharing your thoughts and experiences with this workbook.

By leaving an honest review on Amazon, you help other couples find a guide that may resonate with their own journey. Your feedback, whether it is about an exercise that particularly touched you or an insight that shifted your perspective, can be a beacon for others. Your words might be the encouragement another couple needs to pick up this workbook and work toward a stronger connection.

In your review, you will not only be assisting fellow readers in their quest for a better relationship, but you are also contributing to a larger community, one where couples uplift one another, and together, work toward understanding, trust, and deep connection.

Your journey and insights matter. They have the potential to inspire and support countless others. So, take a moment, if you can, to share your experience. Every voice, every story, and every relationship adds to our collective wisdom.

Scan to leave a review on amazon US

Scan to leave a review on amazon UK

Scan to leave a review on amazon CA

Thank you for choosing to embark on this journey with me. Relationships are the very fabric of our lives, and by strengthening yours, we pave the way for others to do the same. Together, let us continue to build relationships filled with understanding, love, and trust.

CHAPTER 10:
SETTING AND RESPECTING BOUNDARIES

B oundaries, both spoken and unspoken, serve as the invisible guardrails that define and protect the sanctity of a relationship. Venturing into this essential aspect of partnership, you will learn the art of setting clear boundaries that honor individuality while promoting unity. It is not just about drawing lines but understanding why they matter, ensuring they are respected, and adapting them as the relationship evolves. Explore methods to address challenges related to boundaries and strike a balance between independence and interdependence. Armed with purposeful exercises and illuminating insights by the end, you will possess a clear guide for formulating boundaries that reinforce trust, understanding, and mutual respect. Through this journey, cultivate a relationship that places value on both personal spaces and shared moments.

The Importance of Establishing Boundaries

Have you ever experienced the feeling of being overwhelmed by your partner's demands or sensed a loss of your individuality within the relationship? These emotions often arise when boundaries are unclear or nonexistent. Let us explore the significance of boundaries in relationships — invisible lines we draw around ourselves to define our comfort zones. These boundaries are crucial for preserving individuality, ensuring that we do not lose ourselves in the whirlwind of love and companionship. Much like the walls of a house protect its inhabitants, boundaries act as invisible barriers safeguarding our emotional, physical, and mental well-being. In relationships, boundaries extend beyond a simple "no" or keeping a partner at arm's length; they are about mutual respect. Understanding and honoring each other's needs, desires, and limits build trust, understanding, and deeper connections. However, finding the right balance can be tricky. While it is essential to maintain individuality, a relationship also requires togetherness. It is like a dance where both partners move in harmony, sometimes coming close, other times giving each other space. The key is to ensure that neither partner feels suffocated or isolated.

Consider a scenario where one partner enjoys social gatherings while the other prefers quiet evenings at home. Without clear boundaries, this could lead to resentment or misunderstandings. Through open communication and respecting each other's boundaries, couples can find a middle ground, ensuring occasional social events and dedicated time for quiet evenings together.

Incorporating boundaries does not mean building walls or creating distance. It is about ensuring that both partners feel heard, valued, and respected. It is about recognizing that while two people come together in a relationship, they are still individuals with their own needs and desires. So, as you journey through your relationship, remember that boundaries are not restrictions but rather signposts that guide you. They ensure that both partners grow together, not just as a couple but also as individuals. After all, a relationship thrives when both partners feel free, respected, and cherished.

Tip: Start with a simple conversation. Discuss your boundaries, understand your partner's, and find ways to honor them. It is a continuous process, but open communication is the first step toward a balanced and fulfilling relationship.

Navigating Challenges Related to Boundaries

Imagine a scenario where Mary, an introverted individual, needs her quiet time after work to recharge. Her partner, John, on the other hand, is extroverted and thrives on social interactions. He often invites friends over for impromptu gatherings, which, while enjoyable for him, leaves Mary feeling overwhelmed and drained. This situation is a classic example of boundary challenges that couples might face.

Boundaries, while essential, are not always easy to navigate, especially in intimate relationships where the lines can sometimes blur. It is not uncommon for couples to encounter situations where one partner's needs or desires clash with the other's boundaries. Such scenarios can arise from differences in upbringing, personal experiences, or even individual personality traits.

Take, for instance, the concept of personal space. While some might cherish their alone time, others might view extended periods of solitude as a sign of emotional distance. Or consider financial boundaries. One partner might be comfortable with spontaneous spending, while the other prefers strict budgeting. These differences, if not addressed, can lead to misunderstandings and resentment.

So, how can couples navigate these challenges? The key lies in open communication. It is essential to express your feelings and needs without casting blame. For example, Mary could tell John, "I value our social life, but I also need some quiet time to recharge. Can we find a balance that works for both of us?" By framing the conversation in terms of mutual respect and understanding, it becomes a collaborative effort to find a solution.

It is also crucial to be proactive. Do not wait for a boundary to be crossed before discussing it. Regular check-ins can be beneficial, allowing both partners to express any concerns or adjustments they would like to make.

Remember, boundaries are not about keeping your partner out; they are about preserving your well-being within the relationship. They ensure that both partners feel respected, understood, and valued. While boundary challenges are inevitable, with empathy, understanding, and open communication, they can be navigated successfully, leading to a stronger and more harmonious relationship.

Balancing Independence and Interdependence

In the intricate tapestry of relationships, two consistent threads weave through—independence and interdependence. Each partner contributes unique colors, patterns, and textures, creating a shared life. How does one strike the right balance between maintaining individuality and fostering a deep connection with a partner? Imagine a dance where, at times, dancers move in perfect unison, reflecting a deep connection, and at other times, they break away to showcase individual moves, only to reunite harmoniously. This dance mirrors the dynamics of independence and interdependence in relationships. Independence is about recognizing and honoring our individual needs, desires, and boundaries. It is about understanding that we are complete in ourselves and do not need another person to complete us. It is the freedom to pursue our passions, spend time alone, and make decisions that are best for us. On the flip side, interdependence is about recognizing that we are part of a team. It is about understanding that our actions impact our partners and vice versa. It is the mutual respect, trust, and support that allows both partners to thrive individually and as a couple.

But how do boundaries fit into this dance?

Boundaries are the guidelines we set for ourselves and our relationships. They help us define what is acceptable and what is not. When we set clear boundaries, we create a safe space for both independence and interdependence to flourish. For instance, you might have a boundary about spending time alone to recharge. This does not mean you are pushing your partner away; it simply means you are honoring your need for solitude. Respecting this boundary allows you to come back to the relationship refreshed and more present. Conversely, you and your partner might have a shared boundary about spending quality time together every week. This fosters interdependence, ensuring you both prioritize and nurture your connection.   Communication is key. Openly discussing boundaries, understanding each other, and finding ways to honor both create a safe space for both independence and interdependence to flourish. It is not about compromise but collaboration — understanding that while partners are distinct individuals, they are also part of a larger partnership. In the end, the dance of independence and interdependence is a delicate one. But with clear boundaries, open communication, and mutual respect, you can create a relationship that celebrates both your individuality and your shared journey.

Exercise: Boundary Blueprint

Boundary Listing: Use this template to list and define your boundaries in various aspects of your relationship. It is crucial to be honest and specific. An example has been shared to guide you.

Aspect of Relationship	Your Boundary	Partner's Boundary
Time spent with friends	*Prefer to spend one evening a week with friends separately*	*Likes to have a joint outing with friends every other weekend*

After listing your boundaries, reflect on how you feel about them and discuss ways to ensure they are respected. *Boundary:*

How do you feel when this boundary is crossed?

_____

_____

_____

What can we do to ensure we respect this boundary?

_____

_____

_____

Are there any compromises or adjustments needed for this boundary?

Monthly Boundary Check-in: As you grow and evolve in your relationship, your boundaries might change. It is essential to regularly revisit and discuss them to ensure both partners feel understood and respected.

Have there been any instances where a boundary was crossed this month? How did it make you feel?

Are there any new boundaries we need to discuss or old ones that need revisiting?

What steps can we take to better respect each other's boundaries in the coming month?

Remember, boundaries are not about restricting each other but about understanding and respecting each other's needs and feelings. They are a testament to the love, care, and respect you have for one another.

CHAPTER 11:

HANDLING EXTERNAL PRESSURES IN YOUR RELATIONSHIP

E very relationship, no matter how robust, encounters external pressures that can strain its foundations. Whether it is societal expectations, familial obligations, or other outside influences, these factors can test the resilience of a couple. In this chapter, we will explore how to recognize and navigate these pressures, turning challenges into opportunities for growth. Learn strategies to manage external pressures and unite as a couple, emerging stronger in the face of external demands. Through purposeful exercises and insightful guidance, fortify the bonds that will help your relationship remain steadfast amidst the noise of the external world.

Identifying External Pressures

Have you ever experienced the burden of external expectations and opinions, seemingly weighing down on your relationship? This is a common challenge faced by many couples, irrespective of the nature of their connection. External pressures, though subtle, can be persistent and influential, emanating from various sources, and profoundly shaping the dynamics of a relationship.

Envision a couple deeply bonded and in love, originating from diverse cultural backgrounds. One family holds a strong appreciation for elaborate celebrations, while the other places value on more intimate gatherings. As they jointly plan a significant event, they grapple with a dilemma, torn between their own preferences and the traditional expectations of their respective families. This scenario serves as a poignant example of how external pressures can introduce tension into a relationship.

Societal expectations wield considerable influence in shaping our beliefs and actions. Narratives about discovering 'the one' and the curated depictions of relationships on social media consistently present couples with a particular vision of what their bond ought to be. While these stories can inspire, they also have the potential to set unrealistic standards, fostering feelings of inadequacy.

Family dynamics constitute another influential factor. Loved ones may hold specific expectations regarding significant relationship milestones. Even well-intentioned advice from friends might not align with the couple's true desires.

Work environments add another layer of external pressure. Discussions about romantic escapades or life challenges can inadvertently set benchmarks. For those not at these life stages, such conversations can evoke feelings of being outpaced.

It is crucial to remember that every relationship is distinct. What's ideal for one might not be for another. Recognizing these external pressures and understanding their impact is the first step in navigating them, ensuring the bond remains resilient amidst challenges.

Tip: Regularly communicate with your partner about any external pressures you both might be feeling. This open dialogue can pave the way for understanding and mutual support.

Strategies for Managing External Pressures

Facing external pressures from various sources, such as friends, family, work, or societal expectations, can be challenging for a relationship. However, like navigating through a storm, there are ways to move forward without letting these pressures sweep away the strength of your bond. Consider the scenario of Jamie and Taylor, deeply in love but conflicted by their families' expectations. Jamie's family upheld a tradition of Sunday dinners, while Taylor's job demanded frequent weekend travels. The tension was palpable, and they felt torn between family obligations and career commitments. Does this sound familiar? Many couples encounter similar challenges where external pressures test the resilience of their relationship. It is crucial to understand that, while external pressures may be beyond our control, we can control our response to them. Jamie and Taylor, for instance, chose to engage in a heart-to-heart conversation with Jamie's family, explaining the situation and, to their surprise, finding understanding and support. Sometimes, effective communication is all it takes. For pressures that may not have straightforward solutions, here are some strategies to consider:

Stay United: It is easy to let external pressures create a rift between you and your partner. But remember, you are a team. When the world seems to be against you, lean on each other for support.

Open Dialogue: Talk about the pressures you are facing. Understand where your partner is coming from and brainstorm solutions together.

Set Clear Boundaries: It is okay to say no. If certain people or situations are causing undue stress in your relationship, set boundaries. It is not about shutting people out; it is about protecting your relationship.

Seek Outside Support: Sometimes, an outside perspective can be invaluable. Whether it is couples therapy or just a trusted friend, do not be afraid to seek help.

Educate and Inform: Often, misunderstandings are the root of external pressures. Take the time to educate those around you about your relationship choices, fostering a deeper understanding.

Adapt and Overcome: As your relationship evolves, so will the nature of external pressures. Be ready to adapt your strategies as needed.

The Strength of Unity Against External Pressures

Picture this: Two individuals, standing shoulder to shoulder, hands entwined, confronting a strong gust of wind. Alone, they might sway, but together, they stand resolute. This imagery encapsulates the core of a relationship when it presents a united front against external pressures.

We have all encountered that one relative with unsolicited advice or that friend who comments on every decision we make. It is easy to feel cornered, questioned, or even doubted. However, what if, instead of letting these external voices create discord, you and your partner could turn them into opportunities to fortify your bond?

When challenges arise, remember that it is not a battle between you and your partner; it is both of you against the problem. Adopting this mindset transforms challenges into occasions for growth. For instance, when societal expectations press on milestones like marriage or having children, instead of feeling pressured, take a moment to discuss your shared vision for the future. What do both of you genuinely want? And how can you support each other in achieving that?

Being in a relationship does not mean losing your individuality. It means having someone to share your journey with, someone who understands your dreams, fears, and aspirations. When external pressures test your bond, lean on each other. Share your feelings, listen actively, and make decisions that prioritize the relationship's well-being.

Remember, every time you face external pressure and overcome it together, you are adding another brick to the foundation of your relationship. Over time, these collective experiences create an unbreakable bond, a fortress of trust, understanding, and love.

Tip: Next time you face an external challenge, take a moment to communicate with your partner. Share your feelings, listen to theirs, and make a collective decision. This simple act can transform challenges into opportunities for growth.

Exercise: Pressure Point Analysis

Every relationship faces external pressures, whether they come from family, work, or societal expectations. These pressures, if not addressed, can strain your bond. This exercise helps you identify, understand, and navigate these pressures together, ensuring they do not become overwhelming obstacles.

List down the external pressures you both feel are impacting your relationship. An example has been shared below.

External Pressure	Source	Impact on Relationship
Work stress	*Overtime and tight deadlines*	*Less quality time together*

For each pressure listed above, discuss the following prompts:

How does this pressure make you feel individually? How does it affect your interactions as a couple? Are there any positive aspects or silver linings to this pressure?

_____

_____

_____

_____

_____

_____

_____

External Pressure	Action Steps
Work stress	*Schedule regular date nights regardless of work schedules; Consider discussing work boundaries with supervisors*

External pressures are an inevitable part of life, but they do not have to determine the health and happiness of your relationship. By recognizing, understanding, and tackling them as a team, you can transform them into challenges you conquer together, rather than obstacles that drive you apart.

CHAPTER 12:

EXPLORING SOCIAL LIFE AND FRIENDSHIPS IN A RELATIONSHIP

B alancing personal friendships and shared social circles is an art that every couple strives to master. As you journey through this chapter, uncover the nuances of maintaining individual friendships while also nurturing shared social experiences. You will learn the importance of "Us" time and "I" time, ensuring that both are given their rightful space and significance. It is about harmonizing the joys of shared acquaintances with the comfort of individual friendships. With enlightening exercises and discussions, you will gain insights into seamlessly integrating social circles and fostering relationships that respect both shared moments and individual connections. This chapter provides the tools to embrace a social balance that enriches the tapestry of your shared life while celebrating individual threads.

The Balance of 'Us' and 'I'

Picture this: It is a Friday evening, and Jordan is faced with a familiar dilemma. On one side, their friends are gearing up for a night of revelry in the city, while on the other, their partner's friends have organized a cozy game night at home. The choice between a lively evening of dancing and laughter and a more intimate one with board games and deep conversations is a real conundrum. It prompts the question: How does one find the delicate balance between nurturing individual social lives and fostering shared experiences in a relationship? Every relationship is a dance of two individuals coming together, each with their own set of friends, hobbies, and social commitments. While it is natural to want to spend every waking moment with your partner, especially in the early stages of a relationship, it is equally essential to maintain your individuality. After all, it is the unique experiences and stories that each partner brings to the table that enrich the relationship. Recall the time you embarked on a solo backpacking trip and discovered the importance of self-reliance, or the spontaneous art class that unveiled a hidden talent. These individual pursuits contribute not only to personal growth but also to inject fresh perspectives and energy into the relationship.

Conversely, shared social experiences play a pivotal role in fortifying the bond between partners. Whether it is attending social gatherings, traveling together, or simply enjoying a shared binge-watching session, these moments become the building blocks of cherished memories. However, as with many aspects of life, balance is the key. Spending excessive time apart can create emotional distance, while constant togetherness might lead to feelings of suffocation or a loss of individual identity.

Effective communication with your partner about your social needs is essential. Together, you can find a middle ground that satisfies both individual desires and the need for quality couple time. Perhaps designate specific days for personal activities and others for shared experiences. Occasionally, introduce your partner to your circle of friends, and reciprocate by getting to know their friends. This blending of individual and shared social lives ensures that both partners feel fulfilled on both fronts. In conclusion, while the dance of "Us" and "I" can be tricky, with open communication, understanding, and a dash of creativity, couples can navigate the social maze, ensuring that both individual and shared experiences enrich the relationship. After all, it is the blend of "Us" and "I" that makes the journey of love so beautiful and unique.

Integrating Social Circles

E nvision hosting a dinner party where the room buzzes with a mix of your closest friends and those of your partner. The air is thick with anticipation as two worlds collide. The evening could unfold in one of two ways: a delightful blend of shared laughter and newfound friendships, or a series of awkward silences and forced interactions. Merging separate social circles is akin to mixing two different colors of paint — a delicate process where the right mix results in a beautiful shade, while missteps can lead to an unappealing mess.

Introducing Your Partner to Your Friends The first step in merging social circles is introducing your partner to your friends. This can be a nerve-wracking experience. Will they get along? What if they do not? It is essential to choose the right setting for this introduction. A casual brunch or a low-key movie night can be ideal, as they provide a relaxed environment conducive to genuine interactions.

Navigating Group Dynamics Every group has its dynamics, unspoken rules, and inside jokes. When introducing your partner to your group, it is crucial to be mindful of these dynamics. Brief your partner about any sensitive topics to avoid or any quirks particular friends might have. Similarly, when you are a newcomer in your partner's group, be observant, listen more than you speak, and try to catch the group's vibe.

Managing Potential Conflicts Despite best efforts, conflicts might arise. Perhaps a friend feels threatened by the new dynamic or is protective and skeptical about your partner. In such cases, communication is key. Address concerns head-on, reassure your friends about your bond with them, and encourage them to give your partner a chance.

It is important to acknowledge that not everyone will become best friends, and that is perfectly fine. Friendships, like any relationship, are based on personal connections. Expecting every friend to form a deep connection with your partner or vice versa is unrealistic. However, with patience, understanding, and open communication, blending social circles can lead to enriched friendships and a deeper bond with your partner. After all, it is in the blending of these two worlds that new memories are made and the foundation of a shared future is laid.

Nurturing Individual Friendships

Have you ever found yourself immersed in memories with a childhood friend or a college buddy, reminiscing about the good old days? These moments of nostalgia are more than fleeting memories; they are a testament to the deep-rooted connections we form outside of our romantic relationships. While the bond we share with our partner is undoubtedly special, it is equally essential to nurture our friendships.

Picture this: You are at a café, enjoying your favorite latte, with a friend you have known for years. The conversation effortlessly flows, weaving through shared memories and new experiences. This friend, like many others, has been a pillar of support, offering a different perspective during times of feeling lost or overwhelmed. Friendships independent of our romantic relationships play a pivotal role in shaping our identity and emotional well-being.

It is easy to get wrapped up in the cocoon of love, especially in the initial stages of a relationship. Weekend plans, vacations, and even daily routines often revolve around our partner. While this shared time strengthens the bond, it is crucial to remember the individuality that made you unique in the first place. Your personal experiences, the challenges you have overcome, and the friendships you have nurtured have all contributed to the person you are today.

Maintaining individual friendships brings a fresh perspective into your relationship. Every conversation with a friend, every shared laugh, or even the occasional disagreement adds layers to your personality. When you bring these experiences into your romantic relationship, it enriches the bond, offering new topics of discussion and shared activities.

Moreover, individual friendships act as a safety net. On days when you feel overwhelmed or need advice outside the relationship's purview, these friends become your go-to. They offer a listening ear, a different viewpoint, and sometimes, the hard truths that we might not want to hear but need to.

However, like any relationship, friendships require effort. It is essential to set aside time for friends, be it a quick coffee catch-up, a weekend getaway, or even a simple phone call. These moments, though they might seem insignificant, ensure that the bond remains strong and the connection, unbroken.

Exercise: Social Balance Sheet

A thriving relationship recognizes the importance of both individual and shared social lives. While it is essential to have shared experiences, it is equally crucial to maintain individual social commitments. This exercise will help you both strike a balance, ensuring neither aspect is neglected.

Step 1: Listing Social Commitments

Use the templates below to list your individual and shared social commitments.

Individual Social Commitments:

Partner's Name	Activity/Event	Frequency
John	Basketball with friends	Weekly

Shared Social Commitments:

Activity/Event	Frequency
Movie night	Bi-weekly

Step 2: Reflecting on the Balance

Discuss the following prompts together:

How do you feel about the current balance between individual and shared social activities?

_____

_____

_____

_____

_____

Are there any concerns about the time spent on individual activities?

_____

_____

_____

_____

Are there shared activities you would like to introduce or prioritize more?

_____

_____

_____

_____

_____

_____

Step 3: Finding Integration and Prioritization

Brainstorm ways you can integrate individual activities into shared ones or prioritize certain activities to ensure a balanced social life.

Activity/Event	Integration/Prioritization Strategy
Movie night	*Introduce a new genre both are curious about*

A balanced social life, both individually and as a couple, is vital for personal growth and relationship strength. By understanding and respecting each other's needs and finding ways to integrate and prioritize, you can ensure a harmonious and fulfilling social life.

CHAPTER 13:

THE ROLE OF SPIRITUALITY IN RELATIONSHIPS

S pirituality, often an intimately personal experience, has the potential to transform into a shared journey that enhances a relationship. As you engage with this chapter, immerse yourself in the realm of beliefs, rituals, and the spiritual connections that bind individuals together. Whether your beliefs align perfectly, stem from diverse spiritual backgrounds, or fall somewhere in the middle, this chapter serves as a guide through the pathways of understanding and mutual respect. Discover strategies to navigate differences, and find the beauty in shared spiritual practices. Through thought-provoking exercises and discussions, develop a profound understanding of the spiritual dimensions that can elevate a relationship. By the end, you will be empowered to craft a relationship tapestry fortified by the intertwining threads of both shared and individual spirituality.

Shared and Individual Spiritual Beliefs

In moments of quiet reflection, many discover solace in their spiritual beliefs — a personal journey walked alone or sometimes in tandem with a partner. In relationships, spirituality extends beyond shared rituals or joint celebrations; it delves into the profound connections that shared beliefs can cultivate.

Have you ever noticed how a shared prayer or a spiritual ritual can bring a sense of calm amid a storm? Or how a simple meditation session together can strengthen the bond between two people? That is the power of shared spiritual practices. It is like a secret language, a bond that only the two of you understand and cherish. But what happens when two souls, each with their spiritual journey, come together? Can individual beliefs coexist with shared ones? The answer is a resounding yes.

Every individual's spiritual journey is unique, and shaped by experiences, teachings, and personal reflections. When two people in a relationship have individual spiritual paths, it does not create a divide. Instead, it adds layers to the relationship, introducing new perspectives and practices.

Imagine a tapestry, woven with threads of different colors and textures. Each thread represents a belief, a practice, or a spiritual experience. When two people come together, their tapestries merge, creating a richer, more vibrant picture. The individual threads do not lose their identity; they enhance the overall design. However, the true essence of spirituality in a relationship lies in respect. Recognizing and respecting your partner's beliefs, even if they differ from yours, is crucial. It is about understanding that their spiritual journey is as valid and essential as yours. And in this mutual respect, you will find that your bond deepens, transcending the physical and emotional to touch the very soul.

Incorporating shared spiritual practices into your daily life can be a beautiful way to connect. Whether through morning meditations, a gratitude journal, or exploring spiritual teachings together, these shared moments become small islands of peace in the chaos of daily life.

In conclusion, while shared spiritual practices can be a bonding force, individual beliefs add depth and richness to a relationship. It is a dance of togetherness and individuality, where two souls, each on their spiritual journey, come together to create a harmonious melody.

Navigating Spiritual Differences

In the quiet moments of reflection, Jane often found solace in the teachings of Buddhism, while David felt a deep connection to the rituals and traditions of Catholicism. Their spiritual paths, though distinct, were integral to their identities. But when they came together as a couple, these differences became both a challenge and an opportunity in their relationship. Have you ever felt the weight of a spiritual difference in your relationship? It is like two rivers meeting, each with its unique flow and direction. At times, these rivers merge seamlessly, creating a beautiful confluence. At other times, they clash, causing turbulence. But remember, it is in these very clashes that the potential for growth and understanding lies. Jane and David, like many couples, faced the challenge of navigating their spiritual differences. They questioned, "How do we respect each other's beliefs without compromising our own?" The answer, though not always straightforward, began with understanding and open communication.

Respecting Differences: The foundation of any relationship is respect. It is essential to recognize that each individual's spiritual journey is deeply personal. Just as we have our reasons for our beliefs, our partners have theirs. Instead of viewing these differences as barriers, see them as windows into your partner's soul. By doing so, you not only show respect but also foster a deeper emotional connection.

Finding Common Ground: While the specifics of spiritual practices might differ, many spiritual paths share common themes of love, compassion, and understanding. Focus on these shared values. For Jane and David, it was the shared belief in kindness and service to others. By centering their relationship on these shared values, they found a common ground that transcended their spiritual practices.

Growth Through Exploration: Differences in spirituality can be a catalyst for personal and relational growth. Engage in open conversations about your beliefs. Attend each other's spiritual gatherings or read about each other's spiritual paths. This not only shows support but also provides an opportunity to learn and grow together.

In the end, spirituality, in all its diverse forms, is a journey of the soul. When two souls come together, with their unique beliefs and practices, they have the potential to create a relationship that is rich in understanding, respect, and love.

Exploring Shared and Individual Spiritual Practices

In the tranquil hours of dawn, one partner finds solace in a quiet corner of their home, meditating. The stillness, the deep breaths, and the connection to the present moment become a grounding ritual. Meanwhile, the other partner often seeks spiritual connection through solitary walks in nature, feeling a profound bond with the universe amidst the natural surroundings. These individual spiritual practices serve as anchors, offering clarity, peace, and a sense of purpose.

Yet, there are times when they come together in shared rituals. Lighting a candle, and sitting side by side, they express their gratitude for the experiences of the past week and set intentions for the days ahead. This shared spiritual practice evolves into a sacred space, a moment of deep connection amidst life's ever-present chaos.

The Power of Shared Rituals: Engaging in shared spiritual practices can be a deeply bonding experience. Whether it is attending a service, practicing mindfulness exercises, or simply sharing moments of gratitude, these rituals pave the way for a shared spiritual journey. They become touchpoints, moments where individuals can connect on a deeper level, reinforcing their bond and mutual understanding.

Respecting Individual Paths: While shared rituals hold immense power, it is equally vital to respect and honor each individual's spiritual journey. Celebrating the unique spiritual practices of each other is essential. These individual journeys contribute to personal growth, which, in turn, enriches the relationship.

Blending the Two: A harmonious balance exists between shared and individual spiritual practices. While individual journeys offer personal insights and growth, shared practices create collective memories and experiences that strengthen the bond. It is about finding equilibrium, where both individuals feel supported in their paths while also finding moments of shared connection.

In relationships, as in spirituality, the journey holds more significance than the destination. When two individuals embark on this journey together, respecting each other's paths while also finding moments of shared connection, they forge a bond that is both profound and enduring.

Exercise: Spiritual Exploration

Spirituality can be a deeply personal aspect of one's life, and when shared with a partner, it can either strengthen the bond or pose challenges if beliefs differ. This exercise aims to provide a safe space for couples to explore, understand, and respect each other's spiritual beliefs and practices.

Step 1: Discussing Personal Beliefs

Reflect on the following prompts individually and then share your thoughts with your partner:

What spiritual beliefs or practices are important to you? How did you come to hold these beliefs or practices? How do these beliefs influence your daily life and decisions?

Your Reflections:

_____

_____

_____

_____

_____

_____

Partner's Reflections:

_____

_____

_____

_____

_____

_____

Step 2: Shared Spiritual Practices

Are there rituals, practices, or beliefs you both adhere to? How do these shared practices benefit your relationship? Are there new practices or rituals you'd like to explore together?

_____

_____

_____

_____

Step 3: Navigating Differences

Are there significant differences in your spiritual beliefs or practices? How do you currently navigate these differences? What challenges arise from these differences, and how can you address them?

_____

_____

_____

_____

Step 4: Action Steps

Based on your discussions, list down action steps on how to integrate or respect differing spiritual practices in your relationship:

_____

_____

_____

_____

CHAPTER 14:

RECONNECTING AFTER RELATIONSHIP DRIFTS

In the intricate tapestry of every relationship, there are moments of closeness and intimacy, followed by phases of subtle distance and disconnection. This chapter aims to illuminate the nuanced signs of relationship drifts, exploring the natural ebbs and flows that can create a sense of distance between partners. While understanding these patterns is crucial, the true essence lies in equipping yourself with tools and strategies to bridge these gaps and reignite the warmth that initially brought you together. Whether driven by external influences or internal conflicts, this chapter offers insights and practical exercises to guide you back to the heart of your relationship. With enlightening exercises and heartfelt discussions, chart your unique path to reconnection. Embrace the lessons within, and embark on a renewed journey of understanding, closeness, and rediscovered passion.

Recognizing Relationship Drifts

Picture a typical Friday evening — the soft glow of the television casting shadows on the walls, two figures engrossed in separate worlds on the couch. One scrolls through social media, the other immersed in a book. The silence, though comfortable, speaks volumes. Days turn into weeks, and weeks into months, mirroring the emotional distance growing between them.

Relationship drifts are like that silent space on the couch. They creep in unnoticed, often masked by the routines and comforts of daily life. It is not always about explosive arguments or glaring issues. Sometimes, it is the quiet moments, the lack of shared laughter, or the conversations that have turned mundane.

External pressures play a significant role in these drifts. Work stress, family obligations, or even personal ambitions can divert attention from the relationship. Over time, partners might evolve, developing new interests or beliefs. These personal changes, while essential for individual growth, can create a chasm if not shared or understood by the other partner.

Shifts in priorities are another common culprit. Remember the early days of the relationship? The late-night talks, the spontaneous dates, the shared dreams? As time goes on, other aspects of life might take precedence, pushing the relationship to the background.

Recognizing these drifts early on is crucial. It is like identifying a small leak in a boat. Address it immediately, and you prevent the boat from sinking. Ignore it, and over time, it might grow, leading to more significant problems.

So, how does one recognize these subtle signs? It starts with self-reflection. Ask yourself: When was the last time you truly connected with your partner? Not just a casual chat about the day, but a deep, meaningful conversation? When did you last share a dream, a fear, or even a simple joy?

Tip: Set aside regular "relationship check-ins" with your partner. These can be weekly or monthly, but they provide a dedicated space to discuss feelings, concerns, and aspirations. It is a proactive way to address potential drifts and ensure both partners are on the same page.

Strategies for Reconnection

Reconnection is an art, a dance of two souls trying to find their rhythm again. It is not about grand gestures but the subtle, everyday efforts that remind both partners of the bond they share.

Imagine a garden that once bloomed with vibrant flowers but now seems a bit withered. It hasn't lost its potential; it just needs some nurturing. Similarly, your relationship holds the same potential. The first step is to spend quality time together. Not just time, but moments filled with intent. It could be as simple as a walk in the park, where you leave behind the world and its worries, focusing solely on each other.

Communication, as always, is the bridge. But it is not just about talking; it is about listening, truly listening. When was the last time you sat down and just listened to your partner's dreams, fears, or even their mundane day? By doing so, you are creating a sanctuary where both of you can be your true selves.

Memories have a unique way of binding hearts. Revisiting those cherished moments, be it through photographs or places, can reignite the warmth. It is like reading your favorite book; no matter how many times you read it, it always brings joy.

Sometimes, the drift might be more profound than you realize. And it is okay to seek guidance. Couples therapy or workshops can provide you with tools and perspectives that you might not have considered. It is like getting a map for a journey you are about to undertake.

Engaging in activities can also be a catalyst. It is not about what you do, but the joy of discovering or even rediscovering something together. It could be as adventurous as hiking or as calming as a pottery class. The essence lies in the shared experience.

Gratitude, often overlooked, is a powerful tool. In the chaos of life, take a moment to appreciate your partner. It is a gentle reminder of the love, respect, and journey you share.

Tip: Reconnection is a journey, not a destination. It requires patience, effort, and understanding. But the beauty of this journey is in its rewards — a bond that grows stronger with time.

The Role of External Support in Reconnection

In every relationship's journey, there are moments when the path becomes foggy, and the destination seems uncertain. It is during these times that the idea of seeking guidance from outside sources becomes not just beneficial but sometimes essential. External support, in the form of couples therapy, relationship workshops, or even trusted confidants, can provide a fresh perspective, helping couples navigate the complexities of their relationship.

Imagine walking through a maze. While you might have a general sense of direction, there are moments when you hit a dead end or find yourself going in circles. Now, imagine having someone on a raised platform, guiding you, offering you a bird's eye view of the maze. That is what external support can provide — a clearer perspective that is sometimes hard to achieve when you are in the thick of things.

Couples therapy, for instance, offers a safe space for partners to express their feelings, fears, and frustrations. A trained therapist can help identify underlying issues, patterns, or triggers that might be contributing to the drift. They can introduce strategies and exercises tailored to the couple's unique situation, fostering understanding and promoting reconnection.

Relationship workshops, on the other hand, can be a source of both learning and camaraderie. Engaging with other couples who might be facing similar challenges can be reassuring. It is a reminder that you are not alone in your struggles and that with effort and the right tools, reconnection is achievable.

Then there is the value of confiding in trusted friends or family. Sometimes, all we need is a listening ear, someone who knows us, understands our history and can offer insights or advice from a place of love and concern.

However, while external support can be invaluable, it is essential to approach it with an open mind and heart. It is about collaboration, not just seeking a quick fix. It is about understanding that every relationship is a work in progress and that sometimes, we need a little help along the way.

In the end, the goal is clear: to bridge the gaps, to find each other again, and to strengthen the bond that has weathered life's many storms. And with the right support, that journey becomes not just possible but also a transformative experience.

Exercise: Reconnection Roadmap

Step 1: Shared Journaling Prompts

Take a moment to reflect on the following prompts individually, then share your thoughts with your partner:

When did you last feel truly connected with your partner? Describe that moment.

What recent events or stressors might have contributed to the feeling of distance?

What is one thing you miss about your partner or your relationship?

Your Reflections:

_____

_____

_____

_____

_____

_____

Partner's Reflections:

_____

_____

_____

_____

_____

_____

Step 2: Reconnection Rituals

Choose a ritual or activity to do together, aiming to reconnect:

- Cook a meal together, focusing on teamwork and communication.
- Take a walk, hold hands, and discuss your day without distractions.
- Set aside an evening for a "no technology" night, focusing solely on each other.

Which ritual did you choose?

_____

Reflections on the Ritual:

_____

_____

_____

_____

Step 3: Planning Special Time Together

Plan a date or special activity to spend quality time together:

What activity or date would you both enjoy?

When will you do it?

What are you hoping to achieve or feel during this time?

_____

_____

_____

_____

_____

_____

Step 4: Reflections on the Reconnection Journey
After spending time reconnecting, reflect on the following:

How do you feel now compared to before starting this exercise?

What insights have you gained about your relationship and each other?

How can you ensure you maintain this reconnected state?

Your Reflections:

_____

_____

_____

_____

_____

_____

_____

_____

Partner's Reflections:

_____

_____

_____

_____

_____

_____

_____

_____

CHAPTER 15

CREATING A VISION FOR YOUR LONG-TERM RELATIONSHIP

P lanning for the future is an integral part of every lasting relationship. Within this chapter, the focus shifts to the horizon, exploring the importance of having a shared vision and the journey of crafting it together. Whether it is dreams, goals, or aspirations, learn how to align them in harmony with your partner. Dive into the intricacies of adapting and evolving together as life brings its twists and turns. Through engaging exercises and profound discussions, gain clarity on your shared path forward. By the close, you will be better prepared to face life's ever-changing landscape, hand in hand, with a clear and shared vision lighting your way.

The Importance of Shared Vision

In the crisp evening air, two silhouettes found solace on a park bench, their breaths visible in the cold air. One turned to the other and asked, "Where do you see us in ten years?" The question, simple yet profound, sparked a conversation that lasted hours. They spoke of dreams, aspirations, and the life they envisioned together. This was not just a casual chat; it was the foundation for the shared vision that would guide their journey ahead.

Every relationship is a journey; a unique adventure two people embark upon. Along the way, there are milestones, challenges, and countless decisions to make. But have you ever paused to think about the destination? Where is this journey leading you both? The answer lies in the shared vision you create together. A shared vision is more than just a mutual understanding or agreement. It is a guiding force, a North Star, that directs the course of the relationship. It is about aligning dreams, setting mutual goals, and charting a path toward them. When two people share a vision, they are not just coexisting; they are building a life together, brick by brick, memory by memory.

Imagine trying to piece together a jigsaw puzzle without having the final picture as a reference. It is challenging, do you agree? Similarly, in a relationship, without a shared vision, partners might find themselves fitting pieces where they do not belong, leading to confusion and misalignment. But with a clear picture in mind, every piece, every decision, every sacrifice makes sense. It all contributes to the bigger picture. While individual dreams are integral, finding intersections between these aspirations is equally vital in a relationship. It is at these crossroads that the most profound connections are forged, transforming the singular "I" into a harmonious "Us." Remember that evening on the park bench? It was not just about predicting the future. It was about creating it. By discussing and envisioning a shared future, the couple was laying the groundwork for a relationship built on mutual respect, understanding, and love.

So, take a moment. Sit down with your partner, and ask that simple yet profound question, "Where do you see us in the future?" The conversation that follows might just be the most important one you will ever have.

Tip: Regularly revisiting and updating your shared vision can help keep the relationship fresh and aligned with changing aspirations and circumstances.

Crafting a Shared Vision

Crafting a shared vision in a relationship resembles the collaboration of two artists working on a masterpiece. Each artist, with their distinct style and preferences, must discover harmony and balance to cohesively create a piece. In relationships, this harmony is achieved when both partners align their dreams, values, and goals for the future.

During the initial stages of love, the excitement of getting to know one another often eclipses the need for long-term planning. However, as the relationship matures, the significance of having a shared vision becomes more apparent. It goes beyond deciding on the next vacation spot or the color of the living room walls — it involves understanding and aligning on the deeper values and aspirations that will shape the journey ahead.

It is essential to recognize that having individual dreams does not mean they stand in opposition to a shared vision. It is about finding where those dreams intersect, understanding the non-negotiables, and building from there. If one dreams of global adventures and the other of a stable home, perhaps the vision is a home in a travel-friendly location or extended trips spaced out over the years.

Starting this journey requires open dialogue. Questions about the future, aspirations, and dreams should be discussed openly and without judgment. From these conversations, common goals will emerge, forming the foundation of the shared vision. Differences, naturally, will arise. But instead of viewing them as hurdles, they should be seen as opportunities for growth and compromise.

Creating tangible representations of this vision, like a vision board or a written list, can be beneficial. It serves as a daily reminder of the goals set together. And as life evolves, so do dreams. It is crucial to revisit this vision, refining and adjusting as needed.

Ultimately, the process of creating this shared vision deepens the bond between partners. It serves as a testament to the commitment to grow together, celebrating successes, and navigating challenges hand in hand.

Tip: Regularly schedule "vision dates" with your partner. Use this time to discuss and realign your shared goals, ensuring you both are moving in harmony toward your desired future.

Adapting to Life's Changes Together

Life is a series of ebbs and flows, with moments of stillness followed by whirlwinds of change. As individuals, we experience these shifts at various points in our lives. However, when in a relationship, these changes become a shared journey, with both partners navigating the waters together.

Imagine the excitement and nervousness of moving to a new city. The allure of new experiences is thrilling, but there is also the challenge of leaving behind the familiar. Now, imagine making this move with a partner. The decision-making process becomes a joint effort, with both individuals weighing the pros and cons, discussing their fears, and sharing their dreams about the new adventure. Parenthood is another significant life change that couples often experience together. The joy of welcoming a new life is unparalleled, but it also brings about sleepless nights, shifts in responsibilities, and changes in dynamics. The relationship, which was once just about the two of you, now revolves around a tiny human being. It is a beautiful transition, but it is not without its challenges.

Career shifts, too, can have a profound impact on relationships. A partner's decision to change careers or pursue further studies might mean adjustments in financial contributions, daily routines, and even relocation. Such decisions require open communication, understanding, and a willingness to support each other's dreams. In all these transitions, the key is flexibility. Life will not always go as planned, and unexpected changes can throw a wrench in the most well-laid plans. Being adaptable, understanding, and supportive can make these transitions smoother. It is essential to remember that both partners are experiencing these changes, albeit from their perspectives. Regular check-ins, open conversations, and ensuring both voices are heard can make a world of difference.

Moreover, revisiting and, if necessary, reshaping the shared vision can be beneficial. As life changes, so do dreams and aspirations. It is okay for the shared vision to evolve as the relationship matures and as both partners grow individually and together.

Tip: Embrace life's changes as opportunities for growth. While it is natural to feel apprehensive about the unknown, remember that every challenge faced together strengthens the bond. Celebrate the joys, support each other through the trials, and always keep the lines of communication open.

Exercise: Future Vision Board

Step 1: Vision Board

Use the space below to visually represent your shared goals, milestones, and dreams. You can draw, paste pictures, or write down keywords. Think about various aspects of your life together - travel, family, career, hobbies, and personal growth.

Step 2: Reflection Prompts

Shared Goals: List down three major goals you both want to achieve in the next five years.

_____

_____

_____

Milestones: What are some milestones you are looking forward to? (e.g., buying a home, starting a family, celebrating a significant anniversary).

_____

_____

_____

Dreams: Describe a dream or aspiration you both share, no matter how big or small.

_____

_____

_____

Step 3: Discussing Priorities

Which goals or dreams are most important to both of you right now? Why?

_____

_____

_____

Are there any goals or dreams where you have different priorities? How can you compromise or support each other?

_____

_____

_____

Step 4: Action Steps

Goal/Dream	Steps to Achieve

CHAPTER 16:
NAVIGATING FINANCIAL HARMONY

M oney is more than mere currency; it is a reflection of values, dreams, and, at times, fears. As you step into this chapter, you will confront the dynamic role finances play in relationships. Understanding the importance of aligning financial goals and values, you'll explore strategies that foster financial harmony. Beyond budgeting and saving, the focus is on creating a shared financial identity. With targeted exercises and invaluable insights, this chapter equips you to tackle financial challenges and opportunities together. As you turn each page, lay the groundwork for a future where you and your partner not only understand but also respect and nurture each other's financial perspectives.

Navigating Money in Relationships: Understanding the Dynamics

In the initial stages of a relationship, when the air is filled with romance, addressing practical aspects like money can feel awkward. However, long-term couples emphasize the importance of understanding each other's financial perspectives for a lasting and harmonious life together.

Have you ever found yourself in a situation where a casual dinner date turned tense because of a disagreement over splitting the bill? Or perhaps you have felt the strain of not being on the same page about saving for a shared goal, like a vacation or a home. These moments, though seemingly small, can be indicative of deeper financial dynamics at play in a relationship.

Money, in many ways, is more than just currency. It carries with it a weight of emotions, values, and past experiences. For some, it might symbolize security, while for others, it could represent freedom. When two individuals come together, they bring with them not just their bank accounts but also their financial histories, beliefs, and fears.

It is not uncommon for couples to have differing views on spending and saving. One might be a spender, finding joy in purchasing the latest gadgets or indulging in frequent dining out. The other might be a saver, always looking for deals and prioritizing a hefty savings account. These differences, if not addressed, can lead to misunderstandings and resentment.

Yet, within these challenges lies an opportunity — a chance to understand, communicate, and grow as a couple. Conversations about financial beliefs and habits extend beyond money; they explore shared values, dreams, and fears.

Tip: Start with open conversations about your financial background. Understand the experiences that have shaped your partner's relationship with money. It is not about judging or changing each other but about finding a middle ground where both feel understood and respected.

Building Financial Harmony

Have you ever found yourself daydreaming about a cozy house on the outskirts of town or a Mediterranean vacation? Now, consider your partner's dreams. Do they align, or do they sway toward a bustling city apartment or a trek through the Himalayas? Our dreams, big or small, come with a price tag. When two people come together, aligning these financial dreams becomes a unique dance.

Imagine you are at a dance class. You have got the steps down, but your partner? They are swaying to a different tune. That is what talking money feels like for many of us. It is a dance where both partners are trying to find the rhythm. And like every dance, it gets smoother with practice.

Start With a Heart-to-Heart: Remember the first time you shared secrets over a candlelit dinner? It is time to do that again, but this time, let us talk numbers. It is not the most romantic topic, but it will bring you closer in the long run.

Walk Down Memory Lane: Our attitudes toward money often stem from our past. Share stories from your childhood. Maybe you saved up for months to buy that bike, or perhaps money was a constant worry at home. Knowing each other's financial journey can foster understanding.

Dream Together: One evening, sit down with a glass of wine or a cup of tea and talk about your dreams. Where do you see yourselves in 5, 10, or 20 years? Now, weave those dreams into financial goals.

Make It Fun: Budgeting may sound tedious, but it does not have to be. Turn it into a monthly date night. Review your expenses, set goals, and maybe even reward yourselves when you hit a milestone.

Seek Wisdom: If things get tricky, do not shy away from seeking help. Sometimes, an outsider's perspective can offer clarity.

In the end, remember it is not about the money. It is about building a life together, understanding each other's dreams, and finding ways to make them come true. So, take a deep breath, hold your partner's hand, and step onto the dance floor of financial harmony.

Empowering Your Relationship Through Financial Education and Literacy

Imagine a scenario where one partner impulsively splurges on a luxury item, while the other is meticulously saving for a shared future goal. The tension that arises from such situations is not just about the money spent; it is often rooted in a lack of financial education and literacy.

Financial literacy is not just about understanding numbers; it is about understanding each other. When both partners are informed, they can make decisions that reflect their shared values and goals. But how can couples embark on this journey of financial enlightenment together? Firstly, it is essential to recognize that financial education is not a one-size-fits-all. Everyone comes from different backgrounds, with varied experiences and understanding of money. It is okay to start from scratch or to admit areas of uncertainty. The key is the willingness to learn and grow together.

One of the most transformative steps a couple can take is attending financial workshops or seminars together. These sessions often provide valuable insights into budgeting, investments, and future planning. They also offer a safe space for couples to discuss their financial aspirations and fears. Books and online resources can also be invaluable. Whether it is a bestselling book on personal finance or an online course, the shared act of learning can bring couples closer. It is like reading a love story where both of you are the protagonists, navigating the complex world of finance hand in hand. However financial education is not just about external resources. Couples can learn a lot from each other. Maybe one partner is a whiz at budgeting, while the other has a keen sense of investment. Sharing knowledge and skills can be incredibly empowering. Open communication is the cornerstone of this journey. It is essential to create a judgment-free zone where both partners can discuss their financial histories, current situations, and future aspirations. Remember, it is not about pointing fingers or laying blame. It is about understanding and moving forward together.

Tip: Start with a simple joint activity, like watching a financial documentary or reading a finance-related article together. Discuss it afterward. This can be a fun, low-pressure way to initiate conversations about money and begin your shared journey toward financial literacy.

Exercise: Financial Planner

Step 1: Current Financial Overview

Category	Monthly Income/Expense	Notes
Total Monthly Income		
Rent/Mortgage		
Utilities		
Groceries		
Entertainment		
Savings		
Other:		

Step 2: Financial Goals

List down your financial goals in the table below:

Short-Term Goals (within a year)	Long-Term Goals (more than a year)

Step 3: Reflection on Spending Habits

Reflect on the past month. Were there any unnecessary expenses? Any surprises? Write them down.

_____

_____

_____

_____

_____

Step 4: Discussion Prompts

Discuss the following questions with your partner and jot down your collective thoughts.

How do we feel about our current financial situation?

_____

_____

_____

_____

_____

What are our financial priorities for the next year?

_____

_____

_____

_____

_____

CHAPTER 17:

NAVIGATING HEALTH AND WELLNESS TOGETHER

The well-being of individuals plays a pivotal role in the vitality of a relationship, serving as both its foundation and a mirror reflecting the shared bond. This chapter sheds light on the interconnectedness of health and relationships. From supporting each other's wellness journeys to understanding the ripple effects of external factors on collective well-being, you will uncover ways to nurture physical, emotional, and mental health together. Through engaging exercises and thought-provoking discussions, discover how to be each other's pillar of strength during health challenges and celebrate wellness milestones as a team. By the end of this chapter, you will be better positioned to champion a shared commitment to health, ensuring a vibrant relationship for years to come.

The Significance of Health in Relationship Dynamics

Have you ever heard the saying, "When you have your health, you have everything?" It is a sentiment that rings true for many, but have you ever considered how your health, both physical and mental, plays a pivotal role in your relationship? Let us dive into this often-overlooked aspect of partnership dynamics. Imagine two individuals, each on their unique health journey. One might be battling a chronic illness while the other is training for a marathon. Or perhaps one is seeking therapy for past traumas while the other is exploring meditation and mindfulness. These individual paths, while personal, inevitably intertwine when these two souls share a life.

When we are in good health, it is like a gentle breeze on a summer day; everything feels lighter and more vibrant. Our energy levels are high, our moods are buoyant, and we are more likely to engage in activities, both solo and with our partner. This positive energy can act as a catalyst, sparking joy and deepening the bond between partners. On the flip side, when we face health challenges, it can cast a shadow over the relationship. It is not just about the physical pain or the mental anguish; it is about the ripple effects. Maybe it is the canceled date nights because of a sudden flare-up or the strain of seeing a loved one grapple with anxiety. These moments test the resilience of a relationship.

Yet, within these challenges lie opportunities — opportunities for growth, understanding, and unparalleled intimacy. When one partner supports the other through a health journey, it forges an exceptionally strong bond. It becomes a testament to the vows of "in sickness and in health." At the heart of navigating health challenges in a relationship is open communication. Engaging in discussions about individual health goals, fears, and needs creates a path toward mutual understanding. The objective is to establish a safe space where both partners feel seen and heard, irrespective of their health status. Integrating shared wellness activities can be transformative. Whether participating in a weekly yoga session, attending joint therapy appointments, or simply taking a stroll in the park, these shared moments serve to fortify the bond.

Tip: Regularly check in with each other about your individual health and wellness goals. This not only keeps you both aligned but also fosters a culture of care and understanding in the relationship.

Nurturing Each Other's Well-Being

In the early days of a relationship, it is easy to get lost in the euphoria of love, often overlooking the deeper aspects of companionship. One such profound aspect is the mutual journey of health and wellness. As time goes on, the importance of supporting each other's wellness journey becomes evident. It is not just about the occasional reminder to eat healthily or the joint gym sessions; it is about understanding, encouragement, and shared experiences.

Consider a scenario where one partner decides to embark on a quest to lose weight or confront a health challenge. The initial days are brimming with enthusiasm, but as weeks unfold, motivation may wane. This is when the role of the other partner becomes pivotal. A simple word of encouragement, a shared nutritious meal, or even a joint workout session can make a significant difference. It is about being the steadfast support when the other feels vulnerable.

Yet, it's not solely about monumental goals; daily habits wield substantial influence over overall wellness. Whether it's opting for organic foods, practicing meditation, or taking evening walks together, these shared activities not only enhance physical health but also provide opportunities for couples to bond, communicate, and evolve together.

However, it is essential to remember that everyone's wellness journey is personal. While mutual activities are beneficial, respecting individual choices is paramount. If one partner chooses a path different from the other, understanding and respect should be the foundation. It is okay to have different routines or dietary preferences. What is important is the mutual respect for each other's choices. The saying, "Couples who sweat together, stay together," might sound cliché, but it holds undeniable truth. Participating in shared health activities, whether yoga, hiking, or cooking healthy meals together, can fortify the bond. It offers opportunities to create lasting memories, confront challenges as a team, and revel in shared milestones.

Tip: Always celebrate the small victories in each other's wellness journey. Whether it is sticking to a diet for a week, achieving a fitness milestone, or even managing stress better, acknowledging and celebrating these moments can boost motivation and reinforce the bond.

The Impact of External Factors on Health and Wellness

External influences are woven into the fabric of life, impacting our well-being and, consequently, the dynamics of our relationships. From societal expectations and workplace stress to the opinions of friends and family, navigating these external factors is essential. Here is a guide on how to handle them:

1. **Understanding Societal Pressures:** We live in a world where there is a constant barrage of information about what's "ideal". From body image to lifestyle choices, societal norms can sometimes create unrealistic expectations. It is essential to recognize these pressures and discuss them openly with your partner. Remember, your relationship's health is not defined by societal standards but by mutual understanding and respect.

2. **Workplace Dynamics:** Stress from work does not always stay at work. It can seep into our homes and affect our personal lives. Instead of letting it build up, consider setting a "decompression" routine after work. This could be a short meditation session, a quick workout, or even just a few moments of silence. This routine can act as a buffer, preventing work stress from spilling into your relationship.

3. **Handling Peer Comparisons:** "They seem so happy," "Look at their vacation pictures," "Their life seems perfect." In the age of social media, it is easy to fall into the comparison trap. But it is crucial to remember that everyone's journey is different. Focus on building and cherishing your unique relationship story rather than comparing it to others.

4. **Dealing with Family Expectations:** Families, with all their love and concern, can sometimes have strong opinions about our life choices. While it is essential to respect and consider their views, remember that the decisions you make as a couple should primarily revolve around what is best for both of you.

5. **Creating a Safe Space:** Amidst all these external pressures, your relationship should be a sanctuary. Create rituals that allow you both to disconnect from the outside world. This could be a weekly date night, a no-phone rule during dinners, or even a shared journaling activity where you both write about your day and reflections.

Exercise: Wellness Tracker

Prioritizing wellness, both individually and as a couple, is essential for a thriving relationship. When both partners are physically and mentally healthy, they can better support each other through life's challenges. This tracker will help you both monitor your wellness activities and reflect on your journey together.

Step 1: Physical Health Activities

Use the table below to track your shared or individual physical activities:

Date	Activity (e.g., jogging, yoga)	Duration	Notes

Step 2: Mental Health Activities

Use the table below to track your shared or individual mental health activities:

Date	Activity (e.g., meditation, journaling)	Duration	Notes

Step 3: Dietary Changes

Use the space below to note any significant dietary changes or plans you both have decided to adopt:

_____

_____

_____

_____

Step 4: Reflection and Discussion

Set aside some time each week to discuss your progress, challenges, and feelings about your wellness journey. Use the prompts below to guide your conversation:

How do we feel about our health progress this week? What went well, and what challenges did we face?

_____

_____

_____

_____

How can we better support each other in achieving our wellness goals?

_____

_____

_____

_____

What are our wellness goals for the upcoming week?

_____

_____

_____

Connecting More Couples to Strengthened Bonds

Dear Reader,

I genuinely hope that this workbook has offered insights and tools to further enhance the love and understanding in your relationship. Each couple has its unique journey, filled with challenges and joys, and I am honored to have been a part of yours.

Your journey and experiences with this book can be an invaluable guide for other couples navigating their relationship's complexities. By taking a few minutes to share your honest thoughts on Amazon, you might just point someone in the direction of the answers and clarity they have been seeking.

Scan to leave a review on amazon US

Scan to leave a review on amazon UK

Scan to leave a review on amazon CA

As an independent author, each piece of feedback is both a learning opportunity for me and a beacon for potential readers. So, if you could spare a moment to write a review, I would be genuinely grateful. Rest assured, I will be reading every word, valuing both your praises and critiques.

Your voice matters and can be the very encouragement another couple needs to embark on their path to deeper intimacy and understanding.

Thank you for letting me be a part of your journey.

Warmly, Emily Pope.

CONCLUSION

Throughout the pages of this workbook, we have embarked on a profound exploration of what it means to be in a relationship. We have delved into the silent whispers of the heart, the unspoken languages of love, and the intricate dance of two souls navigating life together.

Relationships, in their essence, are more than just shared moments and intertwined fingers. They are the silent promises made in the quiet of the night, the laughter echoing in shared memories, and the strength found in each other during life's storms. They are about growth, understanding, and the continuous journey of rediscovery.

But as you turn this last page, remember that the true essence of this workbook is not in its words but in its application. It is in those quiet moments when you choose understanding over anger, compassion over judgment, and love over indifference. It is in the choices you make, day in and day out, to nurture, cherish, and grow together.

So, as you move forward, I urge you to take these lessons to heart. To not just read them, but to live them. To make them a part of your daily dance. Because in the end, it is not about the grand gestures but the small, everyday choices that build a lifetime of love.

From my heart to yours, I want to share a simple wish: May your relationship be the safe harbor in life's storms and the joy in your every day. As you continue on this journey, remember that love is not just a feeling; it is a choice, an action, a commitment. Choose it every day.

With all my warmth and best wishes, may your journey be filled with love, understanding, and countless moments of joy.

ABOUT THE AUTHOR

Emily Pope is a seasoned writer, known for her insightful and transformative works that delve into the intricate dynamics of human relationships. With a natural flair for capturing the complexities of interpersonal connections, Emily has become a beacon of light for couples seeking to deepen their bonds and navigate the intricate pathways of intimacy and trust.

Emily's journey into the world of relationship dynamics was not born from the halls of academia but rather from the rich tapestry of her own life experiences. Each piece of wisdom, every insight, is carved from the crucible of her own trials, triumphs, and reflections. She has walked through the fire and emerged with a wealth of understanding that transcends conventional learning. In the quiet corners of a bustling city, Emily found her sanctuary in the world of books and writing. Each word she penned was a step toward unraveling the enigmatic dance of human connections. Her writings are not just reflections but are imbued with actionable insights that have proven to be the compass for many who find themselves lost in the labyrinth of love, trust, and intimacy.

Emily's writings are a symphony of her soulful encounters and earnest observations. She believes in the transformative power of communication, the magic that unfolds in the silent spaces between words, and the profound impact of vulnerability. Emily's insights are not just read but are experienced, offering readers a journey into depths of connection they had only dared to dream of. Amid her writing, Emily finds solace and inspiration in the embrace of nature. The rustling leaves narrate tales of enduring love, while the flowing rivers are reminiscent of the ever-evolving nature of relationships. She is an avid traveler, each journey bringing her face-to-face with diverse cultures and stories of love and connection that transcend language and geography.

Emily Pope is not just an author but a companion to those on the arduous yet rewarding journey of building profound connections. In a world where relationships are often lost in translation, Emily's voice emerges as the bridge that not only spans the gaps but celebrates the beautiful imperfections that make every connection unique and sacred.

Printed in Great Britain
by Amazon